amazon.com·

Your order of June 20, 2013 (Order ID 107-5783788-9626652)

Qty.	Item
1	**Bell Plantation PB2 Powdered Peanut Butter, 16-Ounce** Grocery **(** 1-B-3 **) X000FV2E4Z** mon0000006335_usf 850791002079 **(Sold by Tru Inertia)**
1	**Great Lakes Select Honey, Clover, 32-Ounce Bottles (Pack of 3)** Grocery **(** 1-B-3 **) B001E5DZRU** 072223000112
1	**The China Study Cookbook: Over 120 Whole Food, Plant-Based Recipes** LeAnne Campbell --- Paperback **(** 1-B-3 **) 1937856755**

Subtotal
Shipping & Handlin
Promotional Certifi
Order Total
Paid via credit/deb
Balance due

This shipment completes your order.

Have feedback on how we packaged your order? Tell us at www.amazon.com/packagi

10/DBFfY7WlN/-3 of 3-//SP-DNCO/sss-us/7189750/0624-11:00/0622-17:41 Pack Typ

Item Price	Total
$7.70	$7.70
$20.91	$20.91
$16.04	$16.04

g	$44.65
ate	$11.94
	$-11.94
	$44.65
t	$44.65
	$0.00

g.

amazon.com

e : K3

THE
CHINA
STUDY
COOKBOOK

Recipes are based on the research of T. Colin Campbell as presented in *The China Study* (BenBella Books, 2005), by T. Colin Campbell, PhD, and Thomas M. Campbell II, MD. References to page numbers in *The China Study* are based on the first edition hardcover.

Permission granted for use of material in *New Century Nutrition* © 1996, published by Paracelsian, Inc.

Photography by Steven Campbell Disla.

BENBELLA
BenBella Books
10300 N. Central Expressway
Suite 530
Dallas, TX 75231
www.benbellabooks.com
Send feedback to feedback@benbellabooks.com

Printed in the United States of America
10 9 8 7 6 5 4 3 2 1

Library of Congress Cataloging-in-Publication Data is available for this title.
978-1-937856-75-5

Editing by Debbie Harmsen
Copyediting by Shannon Kelly
Proofreading by Brittany Dowdle and Chris Gage
Indexing by Jigsaw Information
Cover design by Kit Sweeney
Text design and composition by Kit Sweeney
Printed by Versa Press, Inc.

Distributed by Perseus Distribution
(www.perseusdistribution.com)

To place orders through Perseus Distribution:
Tel: 800-343-4499
Fax: 800-351-5073
E-mail: orderentry@perseusbooks.com

Significant discounts for bulk sales are available.
Please contact Glenn Yeffeth at glenn@benbellabooks.com or 214-750-3628

THE
CHINA
STUDY
COOKBOOK

OVER 120 WHOLE FOOD, PLANT-BASED RECIPES

LEANNE CAMPBELL, PHD

FOREWORD BY T. COLIN CAMPBELL, COAUTHOR OF *THE CHINA STUDY*

BENBELLA BOOKS, INC.
DALLAS, TX

ACKNOWLEDGMENTS

We went through several steps in putting together this cookbook, one of which involved testing the recipes. The TCC Foundation organized the initial testing process. There were many wonderful people who assisted with testing, including Dan and Becky Mikles, Nancy Porteous, Julia Sokol, Kathy Pollard, Dawn Shepard, Ann Parkin, Patricia Hale, Louann Savage, and Richard Revell. Later the recipes were retested. Amber Gilbert, the wonderful, vegan chef retested several of them. However, I would really like to thank my mother, Karen Campbell, who helped test the recipes throughout the entire process. Once the recipes were perfected, we prepared the different dishes so we could take pictures of them. I would like to thank Steven Campbell Disla, my son, for taking the photographs—sometimes more than 150 pictures for each recipe. I would also like to thank those who assisted in preparing the recipes to be photographed: my mother, Karen Campbell, once again; my sons, Steven and Nelson Disla; and their close friends. They spent countless hours helping make this

book a reality. As Steven said, "God, why do I always smell like onions?"

I would also like to thank those who contributed their own recipes to this cookbook. In particular, I want to thank my sister-in-law, Kimberly Campbell, who has been preparing plant-based meals for more than twenty years. I would also like to thank my mother for contributing her recipes to this cookbook. As we all know, she is AMAZING.

And finally, I would like to thank all the people who provided moral support for this project. Friends, such as Meredith Condor and Beth Silberman, always provided a vote of confidence and encouragement. My family—especially my parents, Karen and Colin Campbell, and my sons, Steven and Nelson Disla—were instrumental in this entire process. Without them, this book would never have happened. Their continual support and encouragement made the whole book possible. And Dad, thanks for always pushing me to stay on track, even when I had other things to do. You guys are the BEST!

51

43

CONTENTS

77

62

110

CONTENTS

BREAKFAST DISHES

APPETIZERS & SALADS

CONTENTS

DESSERTS

APPENDIX

FOREWORD

I am prejudiced, and I might as well say so up front. The author of this book is my daughter, LeAnne Campbell. But, prejudiced or not, I know her style of cooking, her recipes (I've tried many), her commitment to good nutrition, and her ability, as a very busy professional, to prepare quick, nutritious meals.

LeAnne engaged her whole family to assist with this project. Both of her sons were ready and willing to help, and they have now become good cooks in their own right. (Her son Steven also took the photos for this book.) Her mother, Karen, and her sister-in-law, Kim, added a few recipes and helped with the taste testing. And I helped too—with the tasting, that is. The recipes in this book are consistent with the health message of *The China Study*, which my son, Tom, and I wrote. This book is written with the intent of helping people

prepare quick, nutritious meals after a hard day's work.

One of the features of LeAnne's book is her use of recipes that contain no added fat and little or no added salt, and that make minimal, judicious use of sweetening agents. Some folks who cannot quite accept the idea of not using oil or fat in their daily diet may question her no-added-fat strategy, but the scientific evidence shows that we should try to avoid using *added* fat, especially for those who are either at high risk of getting a degenerative disease (which is most people) or who have already been diagnosed with one (e.g., cardiovascular diseases, cancers, diabetes, and other metabolic disorders, and obesity). I am using the term "added" fat in order to distinguish it from whole plant-based foods that are high in fat, because the latter often contain a natural supply of antioxidants, fiber, and the right kind of protein.

I know that for many people who have always eaten the typical American diet, switching to a no-added-fat diet can be challenging—at least at first. But it's important to know that fat has been proven to be addictive, often causing people to consume increasing amounts over time. Eventually, it becomes quite difficult for many people to recover from this addiction. As with any other addiction, some people not only find it difficult to switch, but they can become unusually defensive about their preferences.

But change is possible. It only takes time, perhaps as much as a few months for some individuals. And once that change is achieved, we discover new flavors among whole plant-based foods that we hardly knew existed. Once people arrive at this healthier place, many then discover that if, out of curiosity, they switch back to that old dish floating in fat, they experience some difficulties—perhaps even real intestinal disturbances—or they may find that the old stuff tastes more like a bad dose of grease.

I have often been asked—a few hundred times, I think—what do my family and I eat? Although I try to respond on the spot, I know well that my very limited answers cannot be satisfying to those looking to make real lifestyle changes. Now I am happy to say that there is a cookbook that comes about as close to the real deal for our family as I can imagine. This is it.

—T. COLIN CAMPBELL, PHD

Coauthor of the best-selling *The China Study,* Professor Emeritus of Nutritional Biochemistry, Cornell University

INTRODUCTION

MY JOURNEY TOWARD A PLANT-BASED DIET

What one eats is a personal choice, often based on what each individual finds tasty, satisfying, familiar, or readily available. When people ask me to think about what I eat and why I eat what I do, I have to pause for a minute. My own life experiences and the experiences of the individuals closest to me—most notably those who cared for me as a child—have affected me, just as such experiences affect everyone. When I was a child, it was often my mother who chose the food I was to eat, simply because she cooked and prepared all of our family's meals. We ate these meals with gusto: pork chops served with mashed potatoes and green beans, spaghetti with meatballs, or a large plate of fried chicken. These dinners were often topped off with homemade desserts and ice cream.

It wasn't until my junior year in high school that my diet began to change because of the findings by my father, Dr. T. Colin Campbell, which he later detailed in *The China Study*, an international best seller. Based on his food-related research, he suggested to my mother that our family start following a diet centered more on plant-based foods than on animal-based foods. As a family, we slowly began transitioning toward a plant-based diet. Instead of serving meat as the main course, my mother began to use meat more sparingly, as a side dish or only for added flavor. We changed from eating a large slab of ham with a side of macaroni to having one or two slices of ham cut into small chunks and added to a large casserole dish of scalloped potatoes, serving eight people.

My mother was always an amazing cook; while I was growing up, I loved her cooking. So when I went away to college, I sought out the familiar, comforting foods of my childhood, which often included animal products. Until this point, my food choices had been based solely on my cravings and what I found to be tasty. My college friends and I would order that late-night pizza with extra cheese and sausage, followed by ice cream sundaes smothered in hot fudge sauce. It really wasn't until I graduated from college that I truly began to question why I was eating what I was eating.

In trying to pinpoint the exact instances that led to my transition to a plant-based diet, I can remember a couple of distinct experiences. Upon graduating from college, I was accepted into the Peace Corps. For the first time, I would really be on my own. I was stationed in one of the more rural areas of the Dominican Republic, working directly with impoverished families and their malnourished children. There was one family in particular—and specifically one child—whom I became attached to. Anita was fourteen months old and weighed barely nine pounds. Her grandmother cared for her while her mother was in the city looking for employment. Anita's grandmother often passed by the clinic where I lived and worked.

One day it had been raining, and the grandmother was carrying a few sacks of food that she had bought in town. She had also taken Anita—who had developed a bronchial infection—to the doctor. I could see Anita's grandmother struggling to carry both the food and the child, so I offered to

carry Anita. As we walked the two miles up the mountain back to Anita's home, I could feel her little heartbeat, so close to my chest. At times she was so still. I had to stop and put my ear down close to her face to hear if she was still breathing.

That evening when I returned to the clinic, I stayed in my room. Usually I would have gone to my neighbor's house to play dominoes or just hang out in their kitchen to share stories. But that evening I wanted to be by myself. Earlier that week, I had started reading the book *Diet for a Small Planet* by Frances Moore Lappé—a book that really resonated with me that evening. As I had taken Anita up the mountain, I passed a thousand-acre cattle farm, as I usually did. The owners of this farm lived abroad, and when they returned to the D.R., they stayed in their second home in a high-class tourist area. Those living around the farm never saw any benefits from this farm that occupied so much of their neighborhood. The meat from the cattle was used only to feed a small portion of the local population—those who could afford it. But those who needed it most received nothing. The comforts on the farm far exceeded the conditions within the homes surrounding it. The cattle had ample land to graze on; Anita, her family, and several of their neighbors lived in small, cramped quarters. Large bins of water with proper plumbing and faucets were readily available for the cattle at any time, allowing them an abundant supply of water. Anita's family and their neighbors did not have this same

luxury. To obtain water, they had to walk a long way to the river and then carry it back to their homes in gallon jugs—and even then, the water was often contaminated.

This struck me as being grossly unfair. Looking at this paradox from a humanitarian perspective, I began to question the production of beef. I thought that perhaps I could take one step toward reducing my consumption of animal-based foods so resources could be used more efficiently.

There was another experience during my time in the Peace Corps that made an impact on my dietary choices, this time from an animal-rights perspective. Near the end of my Peace Corps tour, I was stationed farther up the mountain, and I was in the process of helping to build a school. In the field beside my house, there was a small pasture where a goat lived. This goat seemed to be rather curious and attentive to what I was doing. He often came

to the fence to follow me around the yard. I started feeding him some of my kitchen scraps, undoubtedly making him even more attentive. He was the first thing I saw each morning when I went outside, and a neighbor claimed that when I returned from work, the goat would hear my motorcycle, come running to the side of the fence next to my yard, and wait for me. I became attached to the goat, who patiently waited for me each day, morning and evening.

One day I came home and saw something that really disturbed me. As I pushed my motorcycle up the back yard, I looked toward the pasture for the goat. There he was—dangling from the fence. His throat had been cut, and his blood was splattered across my yard. His eyes seemed to be following me as I pushed my motorcycle up the path. Those eyes were no longer smiling; they were pleading, in deep pain, almost begging me to help. But I could not do anything. His blood continued to flow slowly through my yard. I felt sick. I turned and went inside.

Later that evening, my neighbors brought me a plate of goat meat, telling me it was well seasoned. I could not eat it. It was the meat of my friend the goat, and I could not help but see his pleading eyes. This was when I stopped eating meat altogether.

I returned home from the Peace Corps with my own beliefs, from both a humanitarian perspective and an animal-rights perspective. At this time, my father was still conducting his research. And everything he was finding suggested that from a health perspective, eliminating animal-based foods and eating a whole food, plant-based diet was absolutely essential. As stated in *The China Study* (p. 348):

Never before has there been such a mountain of empirical research supporting a whole food, plant-based diet. Now, for example, we can obtain images of the arteries in the heart, and then show conclusively, as Drs. Dean Ornish and Caldwell Esselstyn Jr. have done, that a whole food, plant-based diet reverses heart disease. We now have the knowledge to understand how this actually works. Animal protein, even more than saturated fat and dietary cholesterol, raises blood cholesterol levels in experimental animals, individual humans, and entire populations. International comparisons between countries show that populations subsisting on traditional plant-based diets have far less heart disease, and studies of individuals within single populations show that those who eat more plant-based foods not only have lower cholesterol levels but also less heart disease. *We now have a deep and broad range of evidence showing that a whole food, plant-based diet is best for the heart.*

Never before have we had such a depth of understanding of how diet affects cancer both on a cellular level as well as a population level. Published data show that animal protein promotes the growth of tumors. Animal protein increases the levels of a hormone, IGF-1, which is a risk factor for cancer, and high-casein (the main protein of cow's milk) diets allow more carcinogens into cells, which allow more dangerous carcinogen products to bind to DNA, which allow more mutagenic reactions that give rise to cancer cells, which allow more rapid growth of tumors once they are initially formed. Data show that a diet based on animal-based foods increases females' production of reproductive hormones over their lifetime, which may lead to breast cancer. *We now have a deep and broad range of evidence showing that a whole food, plant-based diet is best for cancer.*

Never before have we had technology to measure the biomarkers associated with diabetes, and the evidence to show that blood sugar, blood cholesterol, and insulin levels improve more with a whole food, plant-based diet than with any other treatment. Intervention studies show that when people who have type 2 diabetes are treated with a whole food, plant-based diet, they may reverse their disease and go off their medications. A broad range of international studies shows that type 1 diabetes, a serious autoimmune disease, is related to cow's milk consumption and premature weaning. We now know how our autoimmune system can attack our own bodies through a process of molecular mimicry induced by animal proteins that find their way into our bloodstream. We also have tantalizing evidence linking multiple sclerosis with animal food consumption and especially dairy consumption. Dietary intervention studies have shown that diet can help slow, and perhaps even halt, multiple sclerosis. *We now have a deep and broad range of evidence showing that a whole food, plant-based diet is best for diabetes and autoimmune diseases.*

Never before have we had such a broad range of evidence showing that diets containing excess animal protein can destroy our kidneys. Kidney stones arise because the consumption of animal protein creates excessive calcium and oxalate in the kidney. We know now that cataracts and age-related macular degeneration can be prevented by foods containing large amounts of antioxidants. In addition, research has shown that cognitive dysfunction, vascular dementia caused by small strokes, and Alzheimer's are all related to the food we eat. Investigations of human populations show that our risk of hip fracture and osteoporosis is made worse by diets high in animal-based foods. Animal protein leaches calcium from the bones by creating an acidic environment in the blood. *We now have a deep and broad*

range of evidence showing that a whole food, plant-based diet is best for our kidneys, bones, eyes, and brains.

More research can and should be done, but the idea that whole food, plant-based diets can protect against and even treat a wide variety of chronic diseases can no longer be denied. No longer are there just a few people making claims about a plant-based diet based on their personal experience, philosophy, or the occasional supporting scientific study. Now there are hundreds of detailed, comprehensive, well-done research studies that point in the same direction.

Armed with my father's research and my own personal beliefs and experiences, I began consuming a diet that was close to being completely plant-based: no animal, meat, or dairy products. I now have two sons who have been raised on a similar diet, as my mother did for me. I have tried to use food not only to nourish them but also to create tasty and healthy dishes.

RAISING CHILDREN TO CONSUME A PLANT-BASED DIET

I am often asked about raising children who consume a strict plant-based diet. Here are some common questions, followed by my answers:

Q. *Do children who are raised on a plant-based diet lack nutrients? How does this diet affect their physical and mental growth?*

Based on the experiences I have had with my sons, I see no evidence that being raised on a plant-based diet has stunted or damaged their physical or mental growth. In fact, it has been quite the opposite. Steven, who is nineteen years old, and Nelson, who is eighteen, are both in excellent physical condition and have always been incredibly active and exceptional athletes, both playing on sports teams since the ages of four and five. Steven is 6'4" and Nelson is a little over 5'11"; both boys are muscular and well-toned. Since entering school, they have consistently earned close to all As and have been very alert and quick-witted. Both have won countless academic and athletic awards. Furthermore, they have rarely been sick. So I would say a

plant-based diet has not harmed them in the least. Instead, it has nourished their mental and physical potentials.

Q. *Where do they get their calcium if they don't drink milk? What do they drink?*

When you consume enough calories from whole plant-based foods, plant foods provide all the calcium you need. It's been an age-old myth that you cannot get the proper amount of calcium from plant-based foods. In place of cow's milk, the boys use rice milk on their cereal; in place of other dairy products in recipes, we substitute soy milk or rice milk. We also use these same products in plant-based desserts and ice cream. With most meals, we drink water. We try to drink at least six to eight glasses of water a day.

Q. *How do your children get enough protein if they don't eat meat?*

When you consume a variety of plants, you will get all the protein you need. Moreover, you will receive a healthier protein

since plant protein is less likely to promote cancer growth and increase blood cholesterol levels associated with heart disease.

Q. *What about when they go to school? How do the other children respond to their diet?*

In school, the boys take their own lunches from home. Often they bring leftovers from dinner the night before or from earlier in the week. They heat their meals up in the morning, before they go to school, and take them to school in insulated containers. If they don't take leftovers, they make sandwiches, several of which are included in this cookbook, such as Delicious Eggless Sandwiches, Hummus Wraps, Granola Fruit Wraps, or peanut butter and jelly sandwiches. When their school friends used to make comments about their food, the boys would occasionally make a game of it. My younger son would call it "the mystery mix" and ask his friends to guess what he was eating. The more different

and strange his food appeared, the more he would enjoy the game. One of his favorite "mystery mixes" was Dominican Beans, served with Fiesta Potato Salad, which has a bright pink tinge from beets.

As is the case with many things in life, it was my sons' attitude toward their dietary preferences, and the fact that they felt comfortable with who they were and why they ate this way, that made it easy for them. Now that they are older, they no longer engage in this game. Often their classmates ask to taste their food, and their friends—much to their own surprise—often want more.

Q. *What do they do when they go to their friends' homes and are offered meat and/or dairy foods?*

My sons' friends and their families respect my sons' dietary choices and have never forced or bullied them into eating meat or dairy products. In fact, their friends' parents' reactions have usually been the opposite: preparing a meat- and dairy-free meal that everyone at the table would enjoy, usually a pasta dish. However, when my sons travel or go on vacation with their friends' families, I will usually pack food for them to take, often rice milk and additional fruit or snacks, sometimes hummus. Their closest friends are actually very accommodating, stopping at fast-food restaurants where everyone finds food that they can enjoy, such as Subway, where the boys can order a vegetable sub, or a restaurant where they can buy burritos, such as Moe's, Chipotle, or Qdoba. Regardless of the specific restaurant, my sons know what they can order.

They have occasionally visited friends who didn't know what to feed them. In these instances, I made sure they ate a meal before going to the friend's house and sometimes packed additional snacks for them to take. It has always worked out, even when we lived in areas of the Deep South, where vegetarianism is rare. During the two years that we lived in a small town in Mississippi, my sons' friends' parents were some of the most accommodating people of all.

Q. *How do you get them to eat vegetables?*

I'm asked this question a lot. I think the answer has to do with the family environment. Children will generally eat the foods that their parents eat. For instance, I

don't like black olives and never use them in cooking. Neither of my sons eats olives. My sister-in-law, however, loves black olives; she cooks with them all the time. As toddlers, her children ate them often. Fortunately for my sons, I love plant-based food, so I have always cooked different dishes with a lot of fresh vegetables, grains, and legumes. This is what they see on a daily basis.

But it's more than what you eat in front of them. It's also important to invite children to help in the kitchen. Have them select a recipe, and if they can, have them prepare the dish, or at least assist you. By being personally involved in preparing meals, children are more motivated to eat what they prepare. As my sons helped with this cookbook and prepared different dishes, they were much more willing to try new food, especially the dishes that they prepared. Dr. Antonia Demas, who has her PhD in education, nutrition, and anthropology from Cornell University, has done research showing that children who prepare their own food are willing to eat their own dishes, even if the dishes contain vegetables that the kids previously disliked. Kids who cook take pride in the food they prepare and will be more excited to try new things. Dr. Demas has created a curriculum called "Food Is Elementary" (available at www.foodstudies.org) based on her research and has worked extensively in schools across the country.

THE GARDEN APPROACH:
CHOOSING A WIDE VARIETY OF PLANT FOODS

THE EIGHT CATEGORIES

One of the interpretations of my father's research was that the consumption of a variety of different parts of whole plants promotes optimal health. Given this, I have broken the plant into seven categories—fruits, grains, leaves, roots, legumes, flowers, and nuts—and given mushrooms a separate category because they can't be

easily categorized as part of a plant. This categorization is to make you aware of the different parts of the plant and to help you think about consuming all parts of the plant. It is not meant to be a strict guideline

but merely a framework to use in trying to put together a meal that Nature deems nutritionally ideal.

We created these categories rather simply. Obviously, roots are the parts of plants that grow below the ground. Leaves include all lettuces, kale, spinach, celery, collards, Swiss chard, cabbage, and so on. Fruits are the parts of plants that contain seeds, such as tomatoes, apples, peppers, cucumbers, pumpkins, and oranges. Grains consist of the seeds themselves: wheat, corn, barley, quinoa, oats, and the like. Legumes are made up of all the different types of beans: soy, pinto, red, black, kidney, and even peanuts. Flowers are broccoli, cauliflower, dandelions, etc. For nuts, I include all tree nuts.

Almost every part of the plant is edible, nutritious, and delicious, and has a different nutrient composition. So it's important to consume a variety of the categories in order to obtain a full complement of nutrients on a given day and across a week or month. To help you with this, throughout this cookbook there are symbols denoting which part of the plant is being used in the recipe (as shown on the next page).

NUTRITIONAL VALUE

Here's a look at some of the nutritional value of the eight categories
(seven types of plant parts plus mushrooms):

FRUITS are packed with vitamin C and other phytochemicals.

GRAINS abound in carbohydrates, fiber, minerals, and B vitamins.

LEAVES are lush with antioxidant vitamins, fiber, and complex carbohydrates.

ROOTS have lots of carbohydrates; some have carotenoids.

LEGUMES are a hearty source of protein, fiber, and iron.

FLOWERS are rich in antioxidants and phytochemicals.

NUTS are loaded with omega-3 fats, vitamin E, and protein.

MUSHROOMS offer a good supply of selenium and other antioxidants.

To be consistent with the message in *The China Study* and especially its sequel, *Whole*,
nutrient compositions are not presented with the recipes. Nutrient contents in different
samples of the same food often are highly variable, leading consumers to be concerned
with trivial and meaningless differences instead of the far more important health
characteristics of food variety and wholesomeness.

CATEGORY	EXAMPLES
FRUITS	ACORN SQUASH, APPLE, AVOCADO, BLACKBERRIES, BLUEBERRIES, BUTTERNUT SQUASH, CRANBERRIES, CUCUMBER, EGGPLANT, GRAPEFRUIT, GREEN PEPPER, KIWI, MANGOES, OKRA, ORANGE, PAPAYA, PEACH, PEAR, PUMPKIN, RASPBERRIES, RED PEPPER, STRAWBERRIES, TOMATO, ZUCCHINI, WATERMELON
GRAINS	AMARANTH, BARLEY, BUCKWHEAT, CORN, KAMUT, MILLET, OATS, QUINOA, RICE, RYE, SORGHUM, SPELT, TEFF, WHEAT
LEAVES	ARTICHOKES, ARUGULA, ASPARAGUS, BASIL, BEET GREENS, BELGIAN ENDIVE, BOK CHOI, BRUSSELS SPROUTS, CABBAGE, CELERY, CILANTRO, COLLARD GREENS, KALE, LETTUCE (ALL VARIETIES), MUSTARD GREENS, PARSLEY, RHUBARB, SEAWEED, SPINACH, SWISS CHARD, TURNIP GREENS
ROOTS	BEETS, CARROTS, GARLIC, GINGER, LEEKS, ONIONS, POTATOES (ALL VARIETIES), RADISH, RUTABAGA, TURNIPS
LEGUMES	ADZUKI BEANS, BLACK BEANS, BLACK-EYE PEAS, CANNELLINI BEANS, GARBANZO BEANS, GREEN BEANS, KIDNEY BEANS, LENTILS, PEANUTS, PEAS, PINTO BEANS, SOYBEANS, WHITE BEANS
FLOWERS	BROCCOLI, CAULIFLOWER, DANDELIONS
NUTS	ALMONDS, CASHEW, HAZELNUT, MACADAMIA, PECANS, PISTACHIO, WALNUTS
MUSHROOMS	BABY BELLA, CREMINI, OYSTER, PORTOBELLO, SHIITAKE, WHITE BUTTON

Adapted from *New Century Nutrition*

Knowing how these nutrients behave in the plant helps us understand how they are used in the human body as well. For instance, roots, seeds, and tree nuts store energy and are generally higher in fat and carbohydrates. They are critical components in starting the next generation of plants, especially in generating plant growth when the weather becomes favorable. If fat is a plant's predominant form of energy storage, as is the case for beans, peas, and tree nuts, that plant will also need to include substances that help prevent the fat from spoiling and becoming rancid through oxidation. The solution to this is antioxidants, such as vitamins and some minerals (e.g., vitamin E and selenium).

Some plants store carbohydrates as a source of energy for their offspring, such as the starch in cereal grains and tubers. These energy-storing foods provide their energy to us as well. In a plant-based diet, about 80 percent of our total energy consumption comes from foods that store most of their energy as carbohydrates and fat. When these energy-containing foods are growing in an environment where they need to be protected from the elements, while waiting for new plant growth they use tough fibers to create a shell-like outer coat, such as the bran layer of grains (this is what we mean by "whole" grains: grains that are milled without first removing the bran). Most plants use fiber to create a rigid structure to keep them erect. We humans use these fibers, many of which we do not digest, to effectively carry our food through our intestinal tracts—a very normal and healthy process.

Because plants use the carbon atom (1) to create the basic chemical structure of organic molecules (fats, carbohydrates, proteins, and vitamins) and (2) to transport energy during its metabolism in our bodies, carbon needs to be "fixed" in the plants. Plants capture carbon dioxide from the air during photosynthesis; the carbon dioxide is then loaded up with energy from sunlight to form carbohydrates. When we humans consume these plants, we oxidize their carbohydrates to release energy for our own use. Photosynthesis, which takes place in the colored part of the plant that is rich in chlorophyll, involves a sensitive energy transfer process that is capable of leaking highly oxidizing chemicals called radicals, which could damage nearby plant tissue. Plants control this potential damage by surrounding the photosynthesis region with layers of antioxidants, like the hundreds (perhaps thousands) of carotenoids, such as beta carotene and lycopene. This is why the colored parts of plants—greens, reds, and yellows—contain so many antioxidants. These substances are very useful for preventing cancers and cardiovascular diseases.

DID YOU KNOW?

One cup of peppers, strawberries, broccoli, or peas all have more vitamin C than one cup of oranges, and one papaya has four times the vitamin C of one orange.

(*The China Study*, p. 302)

Another connection between plant and animal functions concerns the formation and use of protein. This protein molecule is unique in that it contains nitrogen, a basic atom of the amino acids of protein. Both plants and animals need to consume protein (which is to say, they need nitrogen), and they recycle it as an essential part of nature. As they do with carbon dioxide, plants also "fix" nitrogen from the air. Microorganisms living within nodules on the roots of legumes, beans, and peas help to fix the nitrogen into the plants so they can make their protein. These foods, therefore, are rich in protein.

There are many, many other examples demonstrating the dependence of humans on plants and vice versa. Plants gather chemicals from the air, water, and soil to make nutrients that humans and animals use.

Humans break these foods down to extract their nutrients, use them, and then excrete their by-products back into the environment for plants to use. The interdependence of humans/animals, plants, and microorganisms sustains life for all groups. Plants make or gather the nutrients essential for our existence (carbohydrates, proteins, fats, vitamins, minerals). With the exception of vitamin B_{12}, which is made by microorganisms, plants provide all the nutrients that we need, in the right amounts and proportions.

In summary, it is very important to consume a variety of plants to make sure we are getting all the nutrients we need. This book uses the garden approach for all of its recipes, stressing the need to choose a wide variety of plant foods. The next step is to put this great variety of plant parts together into a nutritious meal.

HARVESTING THE GARDEN: PREPARING DELICIOUS MEALS

PLANNING

If you're like me, you probably don't have much time during the week to cook. I often work long hours, and when I come home, I'm exhausted. I want to cook something fast and easy. I've found that a small amount of time invested in menu planning saves me time, energy, and money.

In preparing a menu for the week, I try to incorporate a wide range of plant products, including foods from the seven different plant part categories. Once I have my menu, I make a list of what I need to buy in order to prepare the dishes. I buy only what's on my list. I save shopping time by getting all my ingredients in a single weekly trip. I find that I also save money when I use a prepared weekly menu.

You don't have to prepare a complete menu for every meal. The key meals to plan are the evening meals. For dinners, I prepare a menu with some simple dishes, such as Crock-Pot soups and a couple of dishes that are easy to double. I generally prepare extra food each evening so we will have leftovers for the following day for lunch, so for lunch shopping items I just make sure to have whole wheat or other whole grain bread or wraps for sandwiches, in case we don't have

1) Set aside time to plan a menu for the week.

2) Look through your low-fat cookbooks [such as *The China Study Cookbook*] for recipe ideas (a mix of familiar favorites with a few new recipes each week usually works best).

3) Select three or four main dishes, and plan to prepare enough of each to provide at least two meals (this will provide all your dinners for the week as well as some lunches).

4) Make a list of all the ingredients you'll need for these recipes.

5) Add some fresh vegetables for salads and side dishes.

6) Add foods you'll need for breakfasts and lunches (whole grain breads, whole grain cereals, fresh fruit and vegetables, etc.).

7) Add any staples you might need to restock, including spices. It's helpful to keep a running shopping list on the refrigerator or in some other convenient place in the kitchen where these items can be listed as soon as you use them up, or even better, as soon as you notice that you're getting low.

8) Don't go grocery shopping when you're hungry! Have something to eat before going to the store.

9) Save your menus and shopping lists. You can reuse them or modify them for future menu planning.

enough leftovers. Then I buy plenty of fruit for snacks during the day. One day during the week, usually Friday, is dedicated to leftovers for both lunch and dinner. Breakfasts are usually the same from day to day, so I simply include some breakfast foods on my shopping list.

"You do have important control over the nutritional state of the food that you eat," notes *New Century Nutrition* (1996), a newsletter based on the work done in China and coordinated by Dr. Amy Lanou, Bob Conrow, Christy Cox, Susan Neulist, T. Nelson Campbell, T. Colin Campbell, and myself. "Careful selection, storage, and preparation of your food can make a real difference in your nutritional health." To help you with the selection process, follow these steps laid out by the newsletter when planning a weekly menu:

PRESERVING THE NUTRIENTS: CAREFUL STORAGE AND PREPARATION OF FOOD

After you've shopped, it's important to preserve the nutrients of your food. *New Century Nutrition* notes the following:

Paying attention to how the food is stored and prepared can preserve most of the natural health-giving properties of the food. Probably the best way to eat a tomato is standing in the garden. Pick the fruit, rub it on your shirt to shine it up and dust it off, and then enjoy every juicy, delicious bite while the sun warms your back. While this is nutritionally (and experientially) ideal, it really is not practical for most people on a regular basis. So the next best thing is to choose storage and preparation methods that maintain as much of this freshness, vitality, and nutritional value as possible.

In terms of storage, time and method are both important. *New Century Nutrition* continues:

Generally, the longer the storage time and the higher the temperature, the greater is the loss of nutrients. Storage time includes the time it takes to transport the food from the farm to store, how long it stays in the store, and how long it sits in your home or the restaurant before it is cooked and/or eaten. Especially with fresh produce, the shorter the time between picking and eating, the more nutrients the food retains.

DID YOU KNOW?

When asparagus is kept for two days at room temperature, it loses one-half of its vitamin C? Similarly, corn loses one-half of its sugar and sweetness in just one day.*

* from *New Century Nutrition* (1996)

In terms of storage methods, to retain the nutrients in your healthy foods follow these tips based on the *New Century Nutrition* newsletter:

- Put your fruits and vegetables in the refrigerator: Chilling produce slows down the degradation reactions that destroy vitamins and sugar.
- Keep dry foods dry and store in a cool, dark place: Not allowing moisture to reach foods such as flour and cereal retards bacterial growth.
- Freeze vegetables well: Frozen vegetables often have a higher nutrient content than fresh foods that have been kept for a few days.

food is prepared.

...st-stored foods can ...ls severely decreased ...ods," according to ... "Losses of vitamin ...tamins due to cook-...gh as 65 to 70 per-...n addition to heat, ...ods are affected by ... and light, accord-...rition:

...n (one of the ... to light, so ...ent should be ...ch as possible. ...in C and ...stroyed by ...in air, so it's ... and root veg-...e skins protect ...ainers until you use them. Water-soluble vitamins—vitamins B and C—from cut greens, stems, and roots are readily leached into cooking water; therefore, steaming and microwaving are often preferred cooking methods [for foods high in these vitamins].

Keep in mind that, while all of these storage and cooking considerations are important, what's most important is to choose a variety of whole fresh plant foods as the main focus of your menu!

ADD LESS FAT, SUGAR, AND SALT

New Century Nutrition continues:

Besides choosing methods that maintain the nutrient content of food, we also suggest that you minimize [the addition of] extra fat, salt, and sugar. Both oils and sugar are partitioned foods and, as such, are generally low in vitamins, minerals, and fiber.

To illustrate the effect of cooking methods on nutritional content, let's compare homemade French fries to a baked potato. If you bring home a potato from a local farmers' market in September, keep it until December, then make it into French fries by peeling, slicing, washing, frying, and salting it, you will end up with a food that has a nutrient content more similar to potato chips than to a baked potato. *Homemade French fries from one medium potato have twice as many calories, eighty times as much fat, and nineteen times as much salt as a medium baked potato.*

LESS FAT

New Century Nutrition continues:

Keeping fat intake low is important, because fat adds to the caloric density of the diet (amount of energy it contains), making healthy weight

GOOD—BYE, GREASE!

When you eliminate added fat in cooking, you not only clean your arteries; you will find it easier to clean your dishes as well.

maintenance more difficult. And, more importantly, high fat intake, especially from animal-based foods, increases your risk of high blood cholesterol, heart disease, some types of cancer, and—when it contributes to excess weight—diabetes and hypertension. Considering the many benefits of a low-fat diet, we recommend that you experiment with cooking methods and try adapting recipes to reduce or remove the added fat to find new ways to make your food taste great!

LESS SUGAR

New Century Nutrition continues:

As most people know, minimizing the consumption of concentrated and refined sugar is now known to be important for many health reasons . . . adding sugar to the diet also reduces the amount of nutrient-rich food we eat. In other words, if we fill up on half a roll of Lifesavers, we

won't have room for a juicy orange. While the orange contains sugar, that sugar is in its native or whole food state—whole foods are better sources of energy because they are packed with lots of other nutrients. The orange is much preferable to the caloric equivalent of the Lifesavers because the orange also offers vitamins, fiber, and water, whereas the candy only offers sugar and some artificial flavors and colors . . .

LESS SALT

Salt is zero calories and the body needs it to function. "Why, then, is salt a problem?" *New Century Nutrition* asks and then explains:

Problems occur when the intake of salt gets too high, which can happen all too easily, because the amount of salt needed by the body each day is less than half a teaspoon. For some people who are "salt-sensitive," meaning that their bodies are not very efficient at removing excess salt, too much salt can cause high blood pressure. For everyone, increased salt intake means an increased need for water to clean it out, an increased risk of bloating [or water retention], and, more seriously, an increased risk of stomach and esophageal cancer.

TRANSITIONING TO A PLANT-BASED DIET

PROCESSED AND ANIMAL BASED FOODS

Processed foods, although often considered as a defined class of foods, do not in fact, have a reliable, settled definition. Theoretically, it could mean anything, from the production and initial preparation of foods to the combination of food parts to make products with special properties. For example, do genetic alterations count? Do pesticide and herbicide contaminants count? Does slicing and dicing vegetable and fruits count after being exposed to air oxidation? Does the combining of food parts (sugar, salt, fiber, oil, synthetic antioxidants) to make them tastier and easier to store, transport or prepare count? For this discussion, I will mostly consider processed foods as those food combinations having inappropriate amounts of salt, sugar, fat and, oftentimes, protein, as in convenience store snacks or as in energy-rich desserts (high fat, high refined carbohydrates).

Transitioning from a diet high in animal products to a plant-based diet is a journey. There are certain foods that are made to resemble animal products, and when first transitioning, these foods can be used in their place. For instance, tofu dogs (vegan hot dogs) can be used to replace hot dogs, while soy-based "meat" crumbles, vegan chicken, or bacon substitutes can be used in place of ground beef. However, based on the findings of *The China Study*, I recommend selecting whole plant-based foods in their native state rather than trying to obtain specific nutrients from highly processed foods. This recommendation is based on three important points:

1) Optimal nutrition occurs when we eat food rather than take in nutrient supplements.
2) The closer foods are to their native states—prepared with minimal cooking, salting, and processing—the greater the long-term health benefits will be.
3) Choose locally and/or organically grown produce whenever possible.

The ultimate goal is to move toward a whole food diet while choosing cooking methods, such as those noted earlier, that retain the

COMPARISON OF THREE LUNCHES

WHOLE FOODS LUNCH	LESS PROCESSED LUNCH	ALL PROCESSED LUNCH
RICE AND CORN SALAD (CORN, RICE, NUTS, VEGGIES WITH DRESSING) AN ORANGE OR BANANA	PEANUT BUTTER AND JELLY SANDWICH OATMEAL COOKIES ORANGE JUICE	HOT DOG AND BUN, KETCHUP POTATO CHIPS TWINKIE COLA

COMPARISON OF THE NUTRIENT CONTENT OF THREE LUNCHES

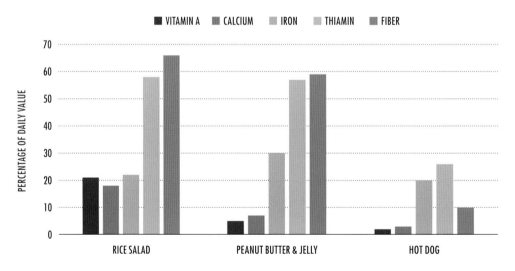

Source: *New Century Nutrition*

HOW MUCH SALT AND CHOLESTEROL IS IN YOUR LUNCH?

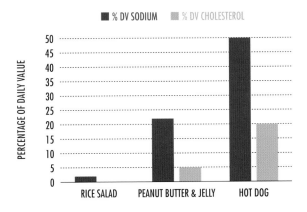

■ % DV SODIUM   ■ % DV CHOLESTEROL

nutritional value of the food and minimize the addition of fat, salt, and sugar. This means that the more processed your meals are, the less healthy they are for you. Take a look at the nutritional values of three sample lunches, ranging from fully processed to minimally processed. The differences in the nutritional breakdown are quite impressive.

THE GREAT EXCHANGE: SUBSTITUTIONS TO CREATE HEALTHY PLANT-BASED RECIPES

Occasionally you may want to change a favorite animal-food-based recipe to a plant-based one (as well as extra-sugary recipes to less refined ones). I have put together a list of possible food substitutions. You may know of other suggestions that work well. Use whatever makes the dish tasty for you and your companions. Be creative and experiment with new spices and flavorings.

MEAT, POULTRY, OR FISH

Depending on the recipe and your food preferences, you can use favorite vegetables, beans, grains, or portobello mushrooms to replace these items. Another food you can use as a substitution while transitioning to a whole food, plant-based diet is tofu, which is available in varying consistencies, from very soft to extra firm (for slicing and crumbling). There is also seitan, a wheat product that comes in plain and spicy flavors, as well as soy hot dogs, veggie burgers, tempeh, and soy crumbles (similar to ground beef).

MILK

Nondairy milks include soy, rice, almond, hemp, cashew, coconut, hazelnut, and many others. Experiment with a few different kinds to find one that works best. Generally soy milk will produce a thicker product, and rice milk a thinner one.

When making a creamy sauce or a pudding, I have found the best replacement to be soy milk. Otherwise, rice milk or any other type of milk substitute can be used in its place.

WHOLE GRAIN FLOURS

There is a wide variety of whole grains, parts of grain (endosperm, bran, cracked), and combinations of grain flours (5-grain, 7-grain, 9-grain) in the market. Wheat, oat, triticale, rye, barley, flax, spelt, brown rice, and durham grain flours are some examples. Use whole grain products, not refined flours.

For some people, their choice of which whole grain (as flour) to use will depend on their sensitivity to gluten, especially found in wheat, barley, and rye. To some extent, determining which grain flour to use in order to avoid this allergy is a matter of trial and error.

EGG REPLACERS

There are many different substitutes you may use for eggs. In most cases, you can use whatever is easiest or more convenient for you without it affecting taste or consistency. Some examples of egg substitutes are: 1 tablespoon ground flaxseed mixed with 3 tablespoons water, 1 tablespoon chia seed meal with 3 tablespoons water, ½ mashed banana, ¼ to ⅓ cup silken tofu, commercial egg replacer used according to the directions on the box, or ¼ cup applesauce—each replacement equals 1 egg. Note that in this cookbook, when an egg substitute is called for in the ingredient list, I use the term "egg replacer."

FATS AND OILS IN MAIN DISHES OR SALADS

Use vegetable broth, water, or wine for sautéing or frying. Or simply bake instead of frying. Try oil-free salad dressings with a base of vegetable broth, water, or vinegar.

PRUNE PASTE

BRANDS WE LIKE

Vegit: an all-purpose seasoning, it can be used instead of bouillon to make broth, as a seasoning for soups, and anywhere you would add dried herbs or spices.

Ener-G Egg Replacer: a common commercial egg replacer that works really well. You should use 1½ teaspoons powdered Ener-G Egg Replacer and 2 tablespoons water for each egg you're replacing in the recipe.

Mori-Nu: This is a great brand of silken tofu. You can find it in most natural groceries or the health-food aisle of your grocery store. It is shelf-stable, so it won't be in the refrigerated section with the regular tofu.

FATS AND OILS USED IN BAKING CAKES, COOKIES, AND SWEET BREADS

Prune paste is one of the best substitutes. It does not change the taste of the dish as much as other substitutions do. Puree 1 cup of pitted prunes in a food processor with ½ cup of water. Substitute ⅓ the amount of prune paste for the amount of oil called for in the recipe (i.e., use ⅓ cup of prune paste to replace 1 cup of oil). Pureed bananas also work well in some recipes, but they do not hold moisture as successfully as the prune paste, and they distort the flavor.

SWEETENERS

When substituting for the sweetness of refined sugar, try concentrated pure fruit juice—specifically apple juice—maple syrup, or any of a wide variety of pureed fruits, including applesauce, bananas, preserves, and jams. Dried fruits, such as dates and raisins, work well for baking. Shredded coconut adds a sweet touch, too.

For sweeteners, there are basically two categories: wet and dry. Here are a few examples of both:

Wet: brown rice syrup, agave nectar, maple syrup, molasses, fruit syrup, barley malt syrup

Dry: date sugar, stevia, raw sugar, turbinado sugar, Sucanat, evaporated cane juice

The sweetness of each sweetener varies, so you may need to alter the amount according to taste. I recommend tasting your recipe along the way to determine if more or less is needed.

SALT

Depending on the recipe, seasonings such as onion, garlic, parsley, coriander, and celery seed can be used. Fresh onion, garlic, lemon juice, salsa, or any type of hot sauce can add zing without sodium (just be careful to check the brand; some are high in sodium). Low-sodium soy sauce is delicious in many recipes.

CHEF'S TOOLS

Every cook has his or her own favorite kitchen tools. Here are some that I use on a regular basis:

Sharp knife and cutting board: This pair is a must-have in any plant-based kitchen. Everyone has his or her favorite knife and cutting board. The great thing about eating a plant-based diet is that you don't need to worry about which cutting board you are using because there is no fear of cross-contamination!

Vegetable peeler: In addition to its regular use, the vegetable peeler can also be used to make thin strips of vegetables for salads and other dishes. It's an easy way to julienne vegetables and also makes short work of peeling butternut squash.

Crock-Pot: Anyone familiar with this appliance will agree with me: it saves time! Many of the soups and stews in this cookbook can be made in the Crock-Pot. Prepare the ingredients and add them to the pot. You will have to adjust the cooking time, but it is a simple and easy way to make a hands-off meal.

Griddle: A pancake griddle isn't essential, but griddles are usually much larger than a regular frying pan, allowing you to make more pancakes at a time. Griddles are usually either electric, so you don't need the stove at all, or the kind that sits on top of more than one stove burner.

Food processor: This kitchen gadget has many uses. Depending on the types of blades or attachments your processor has, you can use it to slice, dice, chop, grate, mix, and/or blend. It is really quite handy. A lot of the time, you can achieve the same results without a food processor, but for some recipes, such as making hummus or pesto, it really is essential.

Blender: This kitchen staple comes in handy, especially when making smoothies or combining liquid ingredients.

START YOUR OWN JOURNEY

The recipes in this cookbook are only a start. As you try them, make note of what works best for you. You may want to modify them, or you might keep them exactly as they are. Each person has his or her own preferences, but sometimes it's fun to experiment. Try new foods and spices you have never used before. When you find something that really works, use those same spices with other dishes. We have found it helpful to have fresh herbs, and each year we try to grow a different herb in our garden.

Don't forget to have fun. As I worked on this book with my sons, I found that we enjoyed our time together in the kitchen. Our lives can be so busy, especially for teenage boys who are active in sports and school events. Sometimes it's hard for all of us to be in the same place at the same time. But as we developed this cookbook, we found that we had quality time cooking together in the kitchen. Now when we are home together during the dinner hour, we all pitch in. It's fun. We pour our favorite beverages and then we cook. We turn on our music or NPR and find that we have some great discussions.

So as you begin this journey, invite your family to join you: your children, your parents, or both. To see pictures of recipes and get additional tips on how to prepare recipes in this cookbook, please visit our Web site at *www.thechinastudycookbook.com*.

Good luck and happy cooking!

—LEANNE

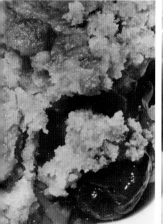

THE RECIPES

BREADS
&
MUFFINS

SWEETENERS AND WHOLE GRAINS

Throughout this and the remaining recipe sections, the non-specific terms "sweetener" and "whole grain" are intentionally used, allowing one to choose their preferred sweetener and whole grain types. Personal preferences vary. Also, for sweeteners, the amount to be used will depend on the sweetness of each sweetener type. Types of sweeteners are listed on page 31, while types of grain flours are listed on page 30. Use of sweeteners should be minimized as much as possible, but refined sugar (sucrose, white table sugar) should not be used. The general theme of *The China Study* is not to be too dogmatic on specific amounts or types of sweetener or whole grain flour, relying instead on personal preference. In some recipes, I have added my own personal preference.

BANANA CRUMB MUFFINS

PREPARATION TIME: 10–15 minutes | **BAKING TIME:** 18–20 minutes
MAKES 1 DOZEN MUFFINS

2 cups whole wheat pastry flour
1 teaspoon baking powder
1 teaspoon baking soda
1 teaspoon cinnamon
2 ripe bananas, mashed
1 cup nondairy milk (rice, soy,
   almond, etc.)
¼ cup Sucanat
¼ cup chopped walnuts

FOR THE TOPPING
6 tablespoons Sucanat (or raw sugar)
½ teaspoon ground cinnamon
¼ cup raw oats (optional)

1 | For the muffins, preheat oven to 375°F.

2 | Line a 12-cup muffin pan with paper liners (or use a nonstick pan).

3 | Combine flours, baking powder, baking soda, and cinnamon in a medium-sized mixing bowl.

4 | In a separate large bowl, mix together bananas (you can mash them right in the mixing bowl), milk, and Sucanat.

5 | Pour the dry ingredients into the wet mixture and stir until well mixed. Add the walnuts, and spoon the mixture into the muffin cups.

6 | For the topping, mix together Sucanat and cinnamon (and oats, if using) in a small bowl. Combine with a fork until crumbly. Press on top of muffins.

7 | Bake in preheated oven for 18–20 minutes, or until a toothpick inserted into the center of a muffin comes out clean. Cool slightly before serving.

BLACKBERRY LEMON TEA CAKES

PREPARATION TIME: 10 minutes | **BAKING TIME:** 45 minutes

MAKES 1 DOZEN TEA CAKES 🍎 🌾

---

2 cups whole wheat pastry flour
½ cup Sucanat
1½ teaspoons baking powder
1 teaspoon grated lemon zest
½ cup plain soy yogurt
1 cup almond milk

1 tablespoon lemon juice
2 egg replacers (2 tablespoons ground flaxseed
  meal with 6 tablespoons water)
1 cup blackberries
2 tablespoons unsweetened reduced fat
  coconut (optional)

1 | Preheat oven to 350°F.

2 | Line a 12-cup muffin pan with paper liners (or use a nonstick pan).

3 | Combine flour, Sucanat, baking powder, and zest in a medium bowl.

4 | Mix together soy yogurt, milk, lemon juice, and egg replacers in a separate bowl.

5 | Pour the wet mixture into the dry mixture and stir until just moistened.

6 | Gently fold in the blackberries.

7 | Spoon mixture evenly into the prepared muffin cups.

8 | Sprinkle coconut over the tops for decoration, if desired.

9 | Bake in preheated oven for 45 minutes, or until a toothpick inserted into the center of a tea cake comes out clean. Cool slightly before serving.

TIPS

Raspberries can be substituted for the blackberries in this recipe.

These tea cakes are delicious served at breakfast.

A HEALTHY WORLD

I often get asked why I decided to switch to a plant-based food diet, and my answer boils down to the simple question: why not? Eating more of Earth's foods in their natural forms not only benefits us, but benefits the world around us too. According to *The China Study*, "By eating a whole food, plant-based diet, we use less water, less land, [and] fewer resources and [we] produce less pollution and less suffering for our farm animals."*

*The China Study, pgs. 239–240

EASY PUMPKIN MUFFINS

PREPARATION TIME: 10 minutes | **BAKING TIME:** 25–30 minutes
MAKES 1 DOZEN MUFFINS 🍎 🌾

2 cups whole wheat pastry flour
½ cup Sucanat
1 teaspoon baking powder
1 teaspoon baking soda
1 teaspoon cinnamon
½ teaspoon ginger
½ teaspoon nutmeg

½ teaspoon allspice
¼ teaspoon salt
8 ounces solid-pack pure pumpkin
½ cup water
⅓ cup applesauce
½ cup chopped pecans (optional)

1 | Preheat oven to 350°F.

2 | Line a 12-cup muffin pan with paper liners (or use a nonstick pan).

3 | Mix together the flour, Sucanat, baking powder, baking soda, and spices in a large bowl. Add pumpkin, water, applesauce, and pecans and stir until just mixed.

4 | Fill the prepared muffin cups to the top and bake 25–30 minutes, until the tops bounce back when lightly pressed. Remove from the oven and let stand 1–2 minutes; then remove the muffins from the pan. Cool for 30 minutes before eating and then store in an airtight container.

> **TIP**
>
> Store cooled muffins in an airtight container in the refrigerator. For longer-term storage, keep them in the freezer.

FIESTA CORN BREAD

PREPARATION TIME: 10 minutes | BAKING TIME: 35 minutes
MAKES 9 SERVINGS 🍎 🌾

1 cup cornmeal
1 cup whole wheat pastry flour
1 teaspoon baking powder
1 teaspoon baking soda
½ teaspoon sea salt
½ teaspoon tarragon

¾ cup corn, fresh off the cob or thawed
⅓ cup unsweetened applesauce
2 tablespoons maple syrup
1 egg replacer (1 tablespoon ground flaxseed
    meal with 3 tablespoons water)
1⅓ cups soy milk

1 | Preheat oven to 350°F.

2 | Place the cornmeal, flour, baking powder, baking soda, salt, and tarragon in a large bowl and mix well.

3 | Add the corn, applesauce, and maple syrup to the dry ingredients and mix. Add egg replacer and milk, and stir until everything is well mixed.

4 | Pour into a 9 × 9 nonstick baking dish.

5 | Bake for 35 minutes or until the top is firm and a knife inserted in the center comes out clean. Cool before serving.

TIPS

Serve with beans and cooked kale or other greens.

If you want a more Italian herb flavor, add 1 teaspoon oregano and 1 teaspoon basil.

LEMON POPPY MUFFINS

PREPARATION TIME: 10 minutes | BAKING TIME: 25–30 minutes

MAKES 1 DOZEN MUFFINS 🍎 🌾

2 cups whole wheat pastry flour
½ cup Sucanat
¼ cup poppy seeds
1 teaspoon baking soda
1 teaspoon baking powder

1 cup almond milk
⅓ cup lemon juice
2 egg replacers (2 tablespoons ground
   flaxseed meal with 6 tablespoons water)
1½ teaspoons vanilla extract

1 | Preheat oven to 350°F.

2 | Line a 12-cup muffin pan with paper liners (or use a nonstick pan).

3 | Stir together flour, Sucanat, poppy seeds, baking soda, and baking powder in a large mixing bowl.

4 | In a separate bowl, mix together almond milk, lemon juice, egg replacers, and vanilla extract. Add the wet mixture to the flour mixture and stir until just combined.

5 | Fill the prepared muffin cups to the top and bake 25–30 minutes, until the tops bounce back when lightly pressed. Remove from the oven and let stand 8–10 minutes; then remove the muffins from the pan.

TIPS

For a stronger lemon flavor, add 1 teaspoon of lemon zest with the dry ingredients.

Chopped walnuts and dry, unsweetened coconut can also be added to this recipe.

RAISIN WALNUT BREAD

PREPARATION TIME: 10 minutes | **BAKING TIME:** 45 minutes
MAKES 1 LOAF

2 cups whole wheat pastry flour
1 teaspoon baking powder
1 teaspoon baking soda
¼ cup maple syrup
1 cup nondairy milk
1 small banana, mashed
1 cup raisins
½ cup walnuts

1 | Preheat oven to 350°F.

2 | Combine the flour, baking powder, and baking soda in a large mixing bowl. Add the syrup, milk, banana, raisins, and walnuts. Stir just enough to mix. The batter will be fairly stiff and sticky.

3 | Spoon into a 9 × 5 nonstick loaf pan and bake for 45 minutes. Remove the pan from the oven and place on a rack to cool.

SENSATIONAL HERB BREAD

PREPARATION TIME: 15 minutes | **RISING TIME:** 1 hour | **BAKING TIME:** 35 minutes

MAKES 1 LOAF

2⅓ cups whole wheat pastry flour
½ tablespoon rosemary
½ tablespoon oregano
1 teaspoon thyme
1 teaspoon basil
1 tablespoon onion powder
½ teaspoon sea salt
2 teaspoons instant (fast rise) yeast
2 teaspoons molasses
1 cup lukewarm water

1 | Combine flour, herbs, and salt in a large mixing bowl. Stir in the yeast.

2 | Make a well in the center of the flour and pour in the molasses and water. Mix by hand to make a soft, slightly wet dough. Knead until the dough leaves the sides of the bowl clean and feels elastic.

3 | Place the dough in a nonstick (small) bread pan, cover with oiled plastic wrap, and leave to double in a warm, draft-free place for about 1 hour.

4 | Preheat oven to 350°F.

5 | Bake for about 35 minutes. Test to see if bread is ready by tapping the top with your knuckles. Bread is done when it sounds hollow.

SEE PICTURE ON PAGE 37

QUICK NO-FAT CRANBERRY BREAD

PREPARATION TIME: 15 minutes | **BAKING TIME:** 45 minutes
MAKES 1 LOAF

2 cups whole wheat pastry flour
¾ cup Sucanat
1 teaspoon baking powder
1 teaspoon baking soda
1 cup orange juice
1 egg replacer (1 tablespoon ground flaxseed
   meal with 3 tablespoons water)
1½ cups fresh cranberries, finely chopped in
   food processor
½ cup chopped walnuts

1 | Preheat oven to 350°F.

2 | Mix together flour, Sucanat, baking powder, and baking soda in a large bowl.

3 | Stir in orange juice and egg replacer. Mix until well blended.

4 | Fold in cranberries and nuts. Spread evenly in a nonstick bread pan.

5 | Bake for approximately 45 minutes or until toothpick inserted in the center comes out clean. Cool for 15 minutes before removing from the pan.

TIPS

If you do not have an egg replacer, you can substitute ¼ cup prune paste (to make a supply of prune paste, mix ½ cup prunes and 1 cup water).

You can also use this recipe to make muffins and serve them for breakfast.

This recipe is great for Thanksgiving and other holidays.

QUICK APPLE LOAF

PREPARATION TIME: 10 minutes | **BAKING TIME:** 30–35 minutes
MAKES 1 LOAF

---

2 cups whole wheat pastry flour
½ cup Sucanat
1 teaspoon cinnamon
½ teaspoon baking soda
1 teaspoon baking powder
½ teaspoon nutmeg
½ teaspoon ginger

¼ teaspoon salt
1 ripe banana, mashed
1 cup nondairy milk
1 teaspoon vanilla extract
½ cup chopped walnuts
1 cup apples, peeled and diced

1 | Preheat oven to 350°F.

2 | Combine flour, Sucanat, cinnamon, baking soda, baking powder, nutmeg, ginger and salt in a mixing bowl.

3 | In a larger, separate bowl, mash the banana, and stir in nondairy milk and vanilla. Mix thoroughly. Add the flour mixture, walnuts, and apples. Mix to combine.

4 | Spread into 9 × 9 nonstick baking pan and bake for 30–35 minutes, until a toothpick inserted into the center comes out clean.

BREAKFAST
DISHES

BLUEBERRY COFFEE CAKE

PREPARATION TIME: 10 minutes | BAKING TIME: 30 minutes
MAKES 8 SERVINGS

1 cup spelt flour
1 cup oat flor
½ cup Sucanat
1 teaspoon baking powder
1½ teaspoons ground cinnamon
½ teaspoon baking soda
1 cup nondairy milk
2 egg replacers (2 tablespoons ground
  flaxseed meal with 6 tablespoons water)

½ teaspoon vanilla extract
1 cup blueberries
¼ cup chopped walnuts

FOR TOPPING
3 tablespoons Sucanat
¼ cup spelt flour
½ teaspoon ground cinnamon

1 | Preheat oven to 350°F.

2 | Combine flours, Sucanat, baking powder, cinnamon, and baking soda in a medium bowl.

3 | Mix nondairy milk, egg replacers, and vanilla extract in a separate bowl.

4 | Pour the wet mixture into the flour mixture and stir until smooth. Fold in blueberries and walnuts.

5 | Spread batter into a 9 × 9 nonstick baking pan.

6 | In a small bowl, combine the flour, Sucanat, and cinnamon. Mix with a fork, and sprinkle topping over batter.

7 | Bake for 30 minutes, or until a toothpick inserted into the center of the cake comes out clean. Cool slightly before serving.

BREAKFAST HOME-FRY HASH

PREPARATION TIME: 10 minutes | **COOKING TIME:** 25 minutes

MAKES 4 SERVINGS

---

4 large potatoes, scrubbed and sliced
6 tablespoons vegetable broth, divided
1 onion, thinly sliced
1 green bell pepper, diced
4 teaspoons light soy sauce or tamari
¼ teaspoon black pepper
6 cherry tomatoes, cut into quarters
2 green onions, thinly sliced

1 | Cut the potatoes into ½-inch cubes and steam them until just tender when pierced with a sharp knife, about 10 minutes. Remove from heat and set aside.

2 | Heat 3 tablespoons vegetable broth in a large nonstick skillet over medium-high heat, and add the onion and green pepper. Cook, stirring frequently.

3 | Add the diced potatoes, 3 tablespoons vegetable broth, soy sauce or tamari and black pepper. Cook, turning gently with a spatula, until the potatoes are golden brown.

4 | Garnish with cherry tomatoes and green onions.

FAVORITE FRENCH TOAST

PREPARATION TIME: 10 minutes | COOKING TIME: 20 minutes

MAKES 8 SLICES

---

1 cup vanilla soy (or almond) milk
1 tablespoon Sucanat
2 tablespoons flaxseed meal (do not mix with water)
1½ teaspoons pumpkin pie spice
1 teaspoon vanilla extract
8 slices whole grain bread
Fresh fruit and syrup, for topping

1 | Mix milk, Sucanat, egg replacer powder, pumpkin pie spice, and vanilla extract in a large mixing bowl to form batter.

2 | Quickly dip one side of the bread into batter and repeat with the second side.

3 | Fry in a nonstick skillet over medium high heat until golden brown.

4 | Serve with fresh fruit, fruit preserves, or syrup.

TIPS

We like to use different types of breads for this recipe (raisin bread is good here).

Instead of fresh fruit, you can use 2 cups of frozen fruit, heated over the stove with 1 cup water and thickened with cornstarch and dry sweetener, as a topping for this recipe.

FRUIT CREPES

PREPARATION TIME: 10 minutes | **COOKING TIME:** 20 minutes
MAKES 4–6 CREPES 🍎 🌾 🥄

FOR THE CREPES
1 cup whole wheat pastry flour
2 egg replacers (2 tablespoons
   ground flaxseed meal with
   6 tablespoons water)
1½ cups nondairy milk

FOR THE FRUIT FILLING
⅓ cup strawberries, sliced
⅓ cup blueberries
⅓ cup peaches, sliced
⅛ cup walnuts, finely chopped
1 teaspoon cinnamon
4 tablespoons maple syrup

1 | For the crepes, place flour in a medium bowl. Mix egg replacers and milk and add to the flour mixture. Beat with a wire whisk until batter is smooth. Batter should be thin. Add more milk if needed.

2 | Heat a nonstick skillet over medium heat until hot. Using a ¼ cup measure, distribute batter evenly over bottom of pan. Tilt and rotate the skillet until batter is spread evenly. Cook the crepe until it is done on the bottom. Flip the crepe and cook briefly on the other side. Remove to a flat plate. Repeat this process with the remaining batter.

3 | If the batter thickens while making the crepes, thin it with a little extra milk.

4 | For fruit filling, mix cinnamon, Sucanat, and fruit in a saucepan over low heat. Stir constantly until sugar and fruit are combined and fruit is lightly cooked. Mix in nuts.

5 | Taking 1 crepe at a time, place 1–2 tablespoons fruit mixture on one side of the crepe. Fold the other side of the crepe over the fruit mixture. Drizzle with maple syrup and sprinkle with cinnamon. Top with fresh fruit.

SAY YES TO CARBS—THE RIGHT KIND

"At least 99% of the carbohydrates that we consume are derived from fruits, vegetables, and greens."* This statistic, as stated in *The China Study*, sounds promising enough. Why, then, are carbohydrates almost always number one on our list of foods to avoid when trying to shed those last five inches off our waistline? In their unprocessed, natural state, foods such as whole grains, fruits, and vegetables are called complex carbohydrates, which are extremely good for you. When foods are highly processed and stripped of their fiber, vitamins, and minerals, however, they are simple carbohydrates—ones found in fatty foods such as white bread, processed snack items, and sweets.

Americans have a habit of consuming large amounts of these simple carbohydrates, and eventually pizza, pasta, fries, chips, and pastries became the poster foods for carbohydrates in general. The truth is that you can eat carbs—just make sure they are the unprocessed, unrefined, and highly nutritious ones found in fruits and vegetables instead.

*The China Study, pg. 98

FRUIT SMOOTHIES

PREPARATION TIME: 5 minutes

MAKES 3 CUPS 🍎

Fruit smoothies have a nutritional advantage over fruit juices because they retain all the fiber that is left out when making juice.

BANANA BLUEBERRY
1 cup frozen banana chunks
1 cup frozen blueberries
¾ cup nondairy milk
2 tablespoons apple juice concentrate

MIXED BERRY PEACH
1¼ cups frozen mixed berries
1⅞ cups sliced peaches, drained

¾ cup nondairy milk
2 tablespoons apple juice concentrate

TROPICAL STRAWBERRY
4 cups frozen strawberries
1 banana
2 peaches
1 cup orange-peach-mango juice
2 cups ice

1 | Place into a blender all ingredients for the fruit smoothie you're choosing.

2 | Blend on high speed, stopping the blender occasionally to move any unblended fruit toward the blades. Serve immediately.

TIPS

For a thinner smoothie, add more milk.

Look for frozen berries in your supermarket, or freeze your own when they're in season.

The secret to making a thick, rich-tasting smoothie is to use frozen fruit.

SEE PICTURE ON PAGE 55

G-MOM'S OATMEAL

PREPARATION TIME: 10 minutes
MAKES 3 SERVINGS 🍎 🌾 🥥

2 cups water
1 cup "old fashioned" oats
½ cup raisins
½ cup blueberries
2 teaspoons maple syrup, divided
½ cup sliced strawberries
1–2 kiwis, peeled and diced
Cinnamon, to taste
Flaxseed
Walnuts, chopped (optional)

1 | Boil water, add oats and raisins, and stir until thick (2–3 minutes).

2 | Place blueberries in the bottom of a serving bowl. Drizzle with 1 teaspoon maple syrup.

3 | Pour cooked oatmeal mixture over the blueberries. Lay strawberries and kiwi on top of the oatmeal. Sprinkle generously with cinnamon and flaxseed, drizzle with 1 teaspoon maple syrup, and sprinkle with chopped walnuts.

TIPS

You can substitute any fresh fruit for the strawberries, blueberries, and kiwi. Bananas and peaches make good substitutes.

My sister-in-law likes to pour rice milk over this oatmeal dish.

PANANA CAKES

PREPARATION TIME: 25 minutes
MAKES 1 DOZEN PANCAKES

2 cups whole wheat pastry flour
1 teaspoon baking soda
1 teaspoon baking powder
½ teaspoon sea salt
1 teaspoon cinnamon
1 banana, mashed

1 cup water
1 cup nondairy milk
2 egg replacers (2 tablespoons ground
   flaxseed meal with 6 tablespoons water)
2 tablespoons maple syrup

1 | Combine flour, baking soda, baking powder, sea salt, and cinnamon in a medium-sized mixing bowl.

2 | In a separate bowl, mix mashed banana, water, milk, egg replacers, and maple syrup.

3 | Combine the wet and dry ingredients, and stir just enough to remove any lumps. The batter should be pourable; if it seems too thick, add more milk.

4 | Preheat a nonstick skillet or griddle.

5 | Using a ¼ cup measure, pour small amounts of batter onto the heated surface, and cook until the top bubbles. Turn with a spatula and cook the second side until golden brown. Serve immediately.

TIPS

Preheat the pan or griddle so that sprinkles of water dance on it, but not so hot that it smokes.

Keep the cakes small. They are easier to turn.

Serve with fresh fruit, fruit preserves, applesauce, or syrup.

MUESLI

PREPARATION TIME: 8 minutes

MAKES 8 CUPS 🍎 🌾 🥥

If you have never tried this granola-type breakfast, then you are in for a real treat.

4½ cups rolled oats
1 cup raisins
½ cup toasted wheat germ
½ cup dried fruit, chopped
½ cup chopped walnuts
½ cup chopped almonds
½ cup unsweetened, reduced-fat coconut (optional)
¼ cup raw sunflower seeds

1 | Combine all ingredients in a large bowl. Mix well.

2 | Store in an airtight container. Muesli keeps for 2 months at room temperature.

TIPS

You can serve this with cold soy milk, or you can add soy milk and heat in the microwave to eat it warm.

As with any cereal, adding fresh fruit (peaches, strawberries, or blueberries) makes it even more delicious.

Feel free to add other flavors you like, such as cinnamon, nutmeg, vanilla, or honey.

NATURE'S GRANOLA

PREPARATION TIME: 10 minutes | BAKING TIME: 1 hour 30 minutes
MAKES 12 CUPS

This is a delicious recipe that makes the perfect ready-to-eat snack!

1 cup water
½ cup packed Sucanat
⅓ cup maple syrup
2 teaspoons vanilla extract
½ teaspoon ground cinnamon
¼ teaspoon ground nutmeg
4½ cups rolled oats

¾ cup wheat germ
½ cup slivered almonds
½ cup chopped cashews
1 cup shredded coconut
1 cup raisins
½ cup dried fruit, chopped

1 | Preheat oven to 250°F.

2 | Add water, Sucanat, maple syrup, vanilla extract, cinnamon, and nutmeg to a large saucepan over medium heat. Cook 2–3 minutes, until sugar is dissolved.

3 | Mix oats, wheat germ, almonds, cashews, and coconut in a separate bowl. Add wet mixture to dry, and mix until coated.

4 | Thinly spread mixture on nonstick baking sheets.

5 | Bake and stir every 15 minutes until golden brown, dry, and crunchy, about 1½–2 hours.

6 | Let cool, and then place in a bowl. Add raisins and dried fruit. Keep in an airtight container for up to 3 weeks.

OUR FAVORITE BREAKFAST BURRITO

PREPARATION TIME: 20 minutes | **BAKING TIME:** 35–40 minutes for potatoes plus 10 minutes for burritos

MAKES 4 SERVINGS

FOR POTATO FILLING
4 large potatoes, diced
Onion powder and sea salt
   to taste

FOR "EGG" FILLING
1 Scrambled Tofu recipe (p. 77)

FOR BURRITOS
4 large whole grain tortillas
1 jar of your favorite non-fat, low-
   sodium salsa
1 15-ounce can black beans
1 package nutritional yeast (optional)

1 | Dice potatoes and bake on nonstick baking sheet for 35–40 minutes at 375°F. Season with onion powder and salt.

2 | While potatoes are cooking, prepare the Scrambled Tofu recipe on p. 77.

3 | Once potatoes and scrambled tofu are cooked, assemble burritos.

4 | For the burritos, place 4 heaping tablespoons of potatoes in the center of the tortilla, top with 4 heaping tablespoons of tofu mixture, and then add 2 tablespoons of black beans. Sprinkle a handful of Daiya cheese or nutritional yeast on top of beans.

5 | Fold the bottom of burrito over, and then fold over both sides.

6 | Once burritos are assembled, place face down on nonstick baking tray.

7 | Bake for 10 minutes at 375°F.

8 | Before serving, spoon 4 tablespoons of your favorite salsa on top. Serve immediately.

PUMPKIN PANCAKES

PREPARATION TIME: 20 minutes
MAKES 1 DOZEN PANCAKES 🍎 🌾

2 cups whole wheat pastry flour
1 teaspoon baking soda
1 teaspoon baking powder
½ teaspoon sea salt
1 tablespoon pumpkin pie spice

2 egg replacers (2 tablespoons ground
   flaxseed meal with 6 tablespoons water)
2 cups nondairy milk
½ cup pumpkin (canned or pureed)
5 tablespoons maple syrup
½ teaspoon vanilla extract

1 | Preheat a nonstick skillet or griddle over medium-high heat.

2 | Combine flour, baking soda, baking powder, salt, and pumpkin pie spice in a large mixing bowl. Set aside.

3 | In separate medium bowl, mix egg replacers, nondairy milk, pumpkin, maple syrup, and vanilla extract.

4 | Combine the wet and dry ingredients and stir just enough to remove any lumps. The batter should be pourable; if it seems too thick, add more milk.

5 | Use a ¼ cup or ⅓ cup measuring cup to measure and pour small amounts of batter onto the heated surface. Cook until top bubbles, about 2–3 minutes. Turn with a spatula and cook the second side until golden brown. Serve immediately.

TIPS

Use a good-quality nonstick skillet or griddle. Some pancakes may be cooked without any fat or oil; others may require a light misting of vegetable oil spray to prevent them from sticking.

Pancakes are best when served fresh and hot. If you want to serve a whole batch at once, keep them warm by stacking them on an oven-proof plate in an oven on low heat.

SCRAMBLED TOFU

PREPARATION TIME: 20 minutes | **COOKING TIME:** 5 minutes

MAKES 4 SERVINGS

---

2 tablespoons vegetable broth
½ large onion, diced
½ large carrot, grated
2 cloves garlic, minced (about 1½ teaspoons)
1 teaspoon curry powder
1½ teaspoons light miso
1 14-ounce package firm silken tofu, crumbled
Sea salt and black pepper to taste
8 chopped cherry tomatoes (optional)

1 | Gently sauté onion, carrot, and garlic in 2 tablespoons vegetable broth in a nonstick pan over medium-high heat until onion is translucent.

2 | Reduce heat to medium and add curry powder, miso, and tofu. Cook, stirring occasionally, for about 5 minutes.

3 | Add salt and pepper to taste. If desired, top with cherry tomatoes and serve hot.

TIPS

Vegit is a powdered, low-sodium form of vegetable bouillon. It can be found in health food stores as well as the health food section of most grocery stores.

This recipe is also good with ½ teaspoon dill.

SCRUMPTIOUS APPLE-FILLED TURNOVERS

PREPARATION TIME: 20 minutes | RISING TIME: 55 minutes
BAKING TIME: 20–25 minutes | MAKES 8 TURNOVERS 🍎 🌾 🥔

FOR THE TURNOVERS
3½–4 cups whole wheat pastry flour
1 tablespoon Sucanat
½ teaspoon sea salt
2½ teaspoons instant (fast rise) yeast
1½ cups warm water

FOR THE FILLING
3 cups apples, diced finely
½ cup walnuts, chopped
¾ cup raisins
2 tablespoons maple syrup
2 teaspoons cinnamon
½ teaspoon nutmeg

1 | Mix all the turnover ingredients together in a bowl. Knead with your hands for 8–10 minutes, until smooth and elastic. Separate into 8 balls; cover, and let rise for 40 minutes.

2 | Once turnovers are covered, prepare filling by mixing all ingredients in a medium-sized bowl and set aside.

3 | After 40 minutes, roll out each ball to a diameter of about 3 inches. Place 1½ heaping tablespoons of filling into the center. For each turnover, fold the edges together to form a half moon. Pinch the edges together with a fork so there are no openings.

4 | Preheat oven to 425°F.

5 | Let your turnovers rise on the counter for 15 minutes.

6 | Place turnovers on nonstick baking sheet.

7 | Bake at 425°F for 20–25 minutes.

TIP
Use a good cooking apple, such as Macintosh, Jonathans, and Cortlands.

APPETIZERS
&
SALADS

BEST BROCCOLI SALAD

PREPARATION TIME: 15 minutes | CHILLING TIME: 2 hours
MAKES 6 SERVINGS 🍎 🥒 🌼 🥜

FOR THE SALAD
1 head fresh broccoli
½ cup dried cranberries
¼ cup red onion, chopped
½ cup walnuts, chopped
2 tablespoons sweetener (agave)

FOR THE DRESSING
3 tablespoons rice vinegar
¾ cup Green Garden Mayonnaise (p. 108)
Sea salt to taste

1 | Cut broccoli into bite-size pieces.

2 | In salad bowl, add broccoli, dried cranberries, red onion, and walnuts.

3 | In separate bowl, mix sweetener, rice vinegar, and mayonnaise.

4 | Pour dressing mixture over broccoli mixture and toss to mix. Season with salt. Chill 2 hours, if time permits.

VITAMIN C IN BROCCOLI

Everyone knows that oranges are a good source of vitamin C. What some of us might not know, however, is that one cup of broccoli has more vitamin C in it than an orange!* While oranges are not an unhealthy alternative, it is always good to balance both fruits and vegetables in your diet. Adding a side of broccoli to your meal is a healthy way to give a boost to your immune system as well as to provide all the nutrients this vegetable is already rich in: vitamin K, vitamin A, folic acid, fiber, protein, potassium, iron, calcium, and many more.

*The China Study, pg. 302

BLACK-EYED PEA SALAD

PREPARATION TIME: 15 minutes | CHILLING TIME: 1–2 hours

MAKES 8 SERVINGS 🍎 🌾 🍃 🌶

FOR THE SALAD

1 15-ounce can black-eyed peas, rinsed
   and drained
2 cups cooked brown rice
2 green onions, sliced
1 green bell pepper, diced
1 celery stalk, diced
2 small tomatoes, diced
1 tablespoon finely chopped fresh parsley

FOR THE DRESSING

4 tablespoons lemon juice
1 tablespoon light soy sauce
¼ teaspoon brown mustard
¼ teaspoon maple syrup
2 cloves garlic, minced

1 | Combine the peas, rice, green onions, green pepper, celery, tomatoes, and parsley in a large bowl.

2 | Mix lemon juice, soy sauce, mustard, maple syrup, and garlic in a small bowl.

3 | Pour dressing over the salad and toss to mix. Chill 1–2 hours if time permits.

TIPS

This salad will keep in the refrigerator for several days and is perfect when you need a quick snack or meal.

For added color and variety, or to add interest to second-day leftovers, add 1 cup of fresh or frozen corn kernels and/or a sweet green or red pepper, chopped.

You can also use cooked fresh, frozen, or dried black-eyed peas in place of the canned peas (use 2 cups).

CELERY SALAD WITH OLIVES

PREPARATION TIME: 15 minutes | CHILLING TIME: 4 hours
MAKES 6 CUPS

6 stalks celery, diced
1 cucumber, diced
1 large carrot, shredded
3½ ounces chopped green olives (or a bit less, to taste)
⅓ cup walnuts, chopped
1 teaspoon garlic powder
1 teaspoon sage
4 cups pasta, cooked (rice, wheat, or whole grain)
½ cup Green Garden Mayonnaise (p. 108)
Sea salt and black pepper to taste

1 | Combine celery, cucumber, carrot, olives, and walnuts in a medium salad bowl.

2 | Mix garlic powder and sage. Pour over the vegetables and toss to coat.

3 | Add cooked pasta and mayonnaise.

4 | Season with salt.

5 | Cover and chill for at least 4 hours or overnight.

CEVICHE BEANS

PREPARATION TIME: 25 minutes
MAKES 3 CUPS

1 medium red onion, diced
1 medium cucumber, diced
2 medium tomatoes, diced
¼ cup cilantro, chopped
1 can white beans, drained and rinsed
1 avocado, chopped
2 limes, squeezed
Pinch of sea salt
Baked low-fat tortilla chips

1 | Combine onions, cucumbers, tomatoes, and cilantro in a medium-sized bowl.

2 | Mix in beans, avocado, and lime juice.

3 | Salt to taste.

4 | Serve with baked tortilla chips crumbled on top.

TIP

Instead of crumbling the tortilla chips, you can keep the chips
whole and serve this as a dip or salsa.

COLESLAW

PREPARATION TIME: 15 minutes
MAKES 4 CUPS

FOR THE SALAD
3 cups finely chopped cabbage
1 carrot, finely chopped
½ red bell pepper, diced
¼ cup dill pickles, diced

FOR THE DRESSING
3 tablespoons vinegar
1 tablespoon agave
2 tablespoons nondairy milk
4 tablespoons Green Garden
   Mayonnaise (p. 108)
½ teaspoon dill
½ teaspoon celery seed
Sea salt and black pepper to taste

1 | Place cabbage, carrot, red pepper, and dill pickles in bowl.

2 | In a separate bowl, mix vinegar, agave, milk, mayonnaise, dill, and celery seed.

3 | Mix dressing with cabbage, carrot, red pepper, and dill pickles.

4 | Add salt and black pepper.

COUSCOUS SALAD

PREPARATION TIME: 20 minutes

MAKES 4–5 SERVINGS

FOR THE SALAD
1 cup quick-cooking couscous
1 medium red bell pepper, chopped
½ cup chopped cucumber
5 tablespoons minced green onion
¼ cup chopped black olives
1 large tomato, chopped
½ cup toasted pine nuts

FOR THE DRESSING
3 tablespoons fresh lemon juice
2 tablespoons water
¾ teaspoon dried oregano
¼ teaspoon dried mint
Sea salt and black pepper to taste

1 | For the salad, in a small saucepan, bring 1¾ cups water to a boil. Remove from heat. Stir in the couscous. Let stand, covered, for 5 minutes. Fluff with a fork.

2 | In a separate bowl, combine red pepper, cucumber, onion, olives, and tomato. Stir in couscous and toasted pine nuts.

3 | In screw-top jar, combine lemon juice, water, oregano, mint, salt, and pepper for the dressing. Screw top on and shake well. Drizzle on top of couscous.

CUCUMBER DILL DIP

PREPARATION TIME: 15 minutes | CHILLING TIME: 2–3 hours
MAKES 5 CUPS

2 small cucumbers
1 pound firm silken tofu
3½ tablespoons lemon juice
2 cloves garlic, peeled
½ teaspoon sea salt
1 tablespoon fresh chopped parsley
1 tablespoon dill
¼ cup finely sliced red onion

1 | Peel and grate the cucumbers.

2 | In a blender or food processor, combine tofu, lemon juice, garlic, salt, parsley, and dill. Blend until completely smooth.

3 | Squeeze grated cucumber to remove excess moisture. Then place in a serving bowl with red onion. Add tofu mixture and stir to combine. Chill for 2–3 hours.

4 | Serve with pita bread or your favorite baked cracker or chip.

TIPS

Reduced-fat tofu works well in most recipes and is available in most health food stores.

Choose tofu that is fresh by checking the expiration date on the package.

SEE PICTURE ON PAGE 81

ENSALADA AZTECA

PREPARATION TIME: 25 minutes

MAKES 8 GENEROUS CUPS

FOR THE SALAD
2 15-ounce cans black beans,
    drained and rinsed
2 cups cooked quinoa or brown rice
½ cup finely chopped red onion
1 green bell pepper, diced
1 large tomato, diced
1 large avocado, diced
2 cups frozen corn, thawed
½ cup mangos, diced

1 jalapeño, finely diced
¾ cup fresh cilantro, chopped

FOR THE DRESSING
⅓ cup unseasoned rice vinegar
2 tablespoons lime juice
½ cup mangos, diced
¼ cup agave
½ teaspoon grated ginger
Sea salt to taste

1 | Combine beans, rice (or quinoa), onion, pepper, tomato, avocado, corn, mangos, jalapeño, and cilantro in a large salad bowl.

2 | In a food processor, place vinegar, lime, mangos, agave and ginger. Process until smooth.

3 | Pour dressing over salad. Toss gently to mix. Season with salt.

TIP

Seasoned rice vinegar has a mild sweet-sour flavor that makes it a delicious salad dressing by itself or mixed with other ingredients.

LOVING LEGUMES

Growing up with an animal-based diet, people tend to think of meat, dairy, and eggs as being the best source for protein. But legumes—such as black beans, peas, green beans, kidney beans, pinto beans, white beans, black-eyed peas, peanuts, and lentils—are also a good source of protein (as well as iron and fiber). In fact, according to *The China Study*, "there is a mountain of compelling research showing that 'low-quality' plant protein, which allows for slow but steady synthesis of new proteins, is the healthiest type of protein."*

*The China Study, pgs. 30–31

FIESTA POTATO SALAD

PREPARATION TIME: 30 minutes
MAKES 6 CUPS

4 large potatoes, peeled and diced
1 pound beets, diced
1 cup carrots, diced
7 tablespoons Green Garden Mayonnaise (p. 108)
1 red onion, diced
¼ cup vinegar
Sea salt to taste

1 | Boil potatoes, beets, and carrots in large saucepan. Drain vegetables and cool to room temperature. Place in a large bowl.

2 | Add mayonnaise, onions, and vinegar to vegetables. Mix until vegetables are covered.

3 | Season with salt. If necessary (depending on your preferences), add more vinegar and/or mayonnaise.

TIP

This potato salad goes well with Dominican Beans (p. 170).

FRESH TOMATO AND AVOCADO PASTA SALAD

PREPARATION TIME: 25 minutes

MAKES 8 SERVINGS

3 cups whole wheat pasta shells, cooked
¼ cup diced red onions
2½ cups cherry tomatoes, quartered
1 15-ounce can chickpeas, drained and rinsed
½ cup basil leaves, finely chopped
2 avocados, diced
1½ cups cooked corn
¼ cup Green Garden Mayonnaise (p. 108)
Sea salt to taste

1 | Cook pasta according to package directions.

2 | In a large bowl, combine onions, tomatoes, chickpeas, basil, avocado, and corn. Add cooked pasta and mayonnaise, and season with salt.

3 | Chill and serve cold.

GREEK SALAD WITH NUTS

PREPARATION TIME: 1 hour

MAKES 6–8 SERVINGS

FOR THE SALAD
6 cups salad greens
1 red onion, diced
1 red bell pepper, seeded and diced
½ cup cherry tomatoes, quartered
1 large cucumber, sliced
¼ cup chopped black olives
¼–½ cup pine nuts or chopped walnuts

FOR THE DRESSING
½ block extra firm tofu, crumbled
½ cup red wine vinegar
2 teaspoons lemon juice
½ teaspoon salt
1 teaspoon oregano
¼ teaspoon thyme
¼ teaspoon black pepper

1 | Combine salad greens, onion, pepper, tomato, cucumber, olives, and nuts in a large salad bowl.

2 | For dressing, mix all ingredients in a bowl and allow tofu to marinate for 1 hour.

3 | Pour prepared dressing over salad and toss to coat.

LEMON TAHINI QUINOA SALAD

PREPARATION TIME: 25 minutes
MAKES 6–8 SERVINGS 🍎 🌾 🥕 🌿 🌼

FOR THE SALAD
2 cups water
1 cup quinoa, uncooked
½ red onion, finely diced
1 cup chopped broccoli
1 medium red bell pepper, seeded and diced
1 medium yellow bell pepper, seeded and diced
2 tomatoes, diced
1 15-ounce can chickpeas

FOR THE SAUCE
¼ cup tahini
3 tablespoons fresh lemon juice
2 tablespoons hot water
2 tablespoons (low sodium) tamari
2 teaspoons sweetener
1 teaspoon powdered garlic
Sea salt to taste

1 | Heat 2 cups water and quinoa until boiling in medium saucepan over high heat. Reduce heat to medium-low and simmer until water is absorbed and quinoa fluffs up, about 15 minutes. Quinoa is done when it is tender and there is a pop to each bite. Drain water and place quinoa in mixing bowl.

2 | Add onion, broccoli, peppers, tomatoes, and chickpeas.

3 | To make the sauce, whisk together all the ingredients.

4 | Add the sauce to the cooked quinoa and vegetables.

5 | Serve garnished with a bit of cilantro.

TIPS

For added color and variety, or to add interest to second-day leftovers, add 1 cup of fresh corn.

This salad will keep in the refrigerator for several days and is perfect when you need a quick snack or meal.

LETTUCE WRAPS

PREPARATION TIME: 25 minutes
MAKES 10 WRAPS

1 head Bibb lettuce
½ cup vegetable broth
3 cloves garlic, minced
1 tablespoon diced fresh ginger
½ medium onion, diced
1 large carrot, grated or thinly sliced
1 celery stalk, finely chopped
1 cup water chestnuts, diced
2 tablespoons sesame seeds
¼ cup light soy sauce
2 cups cooked bulgur

2 tablespoons nutritional yeast
1 teaspoon thyme, dried leaves
Sea salt and black pepper to taste

PEANUT DRESSING
¼ cup natural peanut butter
1 tablespoon soy sauce or tamari
½ teaspoon ginger, grated
¼ cup Mae Ploy
¼ cup coconut milk, lite

1 | Wash lettuce leaves, pat dry, and set aside.

2 | In a medium skillet, add vegetable broth, garlic, ginger, onion, carrot, celery, and water chestnuts. Cook over medium-high heat until onion is translucent.

3 | Add sesame seeds, soy sauce, and bulgur. Stir fry for 1–2 minutes.

4 | Remove from heat, stir in nutritional yeast and thyme, and season with salt and pepper.

5 | For peanut dressing, whisk together all ingredients.

6 | Take a whole lettuce leaf and place 2–3 tablespoons of filling in the center. Add 1 tablespoon peanut dressing. Roll into a wrap and enjoy.

TIP

Mae Ploy is a Thai curry paste and can be purchased in the Asian/International section of most grocery stores.

GREEN GARDEN MAYONNAISE

PREPARATION TIME: 10 minutes

MAKES 1 CUP

---

6 ounces firm silken tofu
¼ cup raw cashews
2 tablespoons lemon juice
1 teaspoon rice vinegar
2 tablespoons apple cider vinegar
1 teaspoon agave
¼ teaspoon sea salt
½ teaspoon Dijon mustard

1 | Blend all ingredients in a food processor until smooth. If you desire a thinner consistency, you may want to blend in a little water.

2 | Refrigerate until ready to use.

TIP

Nutritional yeast, which can be purchased in health food stores, adds a slight nutty and cheesy flavor. If desired, add 1 teaspoon.

MEXICAN JICAMA SALAD

PREPARATION TIME: 15 minutes

MAKES 6–8 SERVINGS

Jicama is also known as the Mexican potato or the Mexican turnip. The root's exterior is yellow and papery, and the inside resembles a raw potato or pear. The flavor is sweet and starchy, and it is usually eaten raw.

FOR THE SALAD
1 medium jicama root, julienned
1 medium carrot, peeled and julienned
½ red pepper, julienned
½ yellow pepper, julienned
1 tomato julienned
1 small red onion, julienned
½ cup cilantro, chopped

FOR THE DRESSING
2 tablespoons seasoned rice vinegar
2 tablespoons lime juice
1 teaspoon stone-ground mustard
¼ teaspoon sea salt
Pinch of cayenne pepper
Pinch of paprika

1 | Combine jicama, carrot, peppers, tomato, onion, and cilantro in a large salad bowl.

2 | In a small bowl, mix the remaining ingredients. Pour over the vegetables and toss to mix.

SAMOSAS BAKED TO PERFECTION

PREPARATION TIME: 20 minutes | RISING TIME: 45 minutes

BAKING TIME: 15–20 minutes | MAKES 6 SAMOSAS

FOR THE PASTRY
3½–4 cups whole wheat pastry flour
1 tablespoon agave
½ teaspoon sea salt
2½ teaspoons instant (fast rise) yeast
1½ cups warm water

FOR THE FILLING
¼ cup vegetable broth, divided
1 medium onion, chopped

2 teaspoons low-sodium Vegit seasoning
1 jalapeño pepper, diced
1 tablespoon minced fresh ginger
1 teaspoon ground coriander
1 teaspoon ground cumin
½ teaspoon turmeric
3 medium potatoes, boiled, peeled,
    and diced
1 cup cooked peas or edamame
1 teaspoon sea salt

1 | To prepare pastry, mix all the pastry ingredients in a bowl. Knead with your hands for 8–10 minutes until smooth and elastic. Separate into 16 balls; cover and let rise for 45 minutes.

2 | While pastry is covered, prepare filling by adding 2 tablespoons vegetable broth to a large skillet over medium-high heat. Add onion, Vegit, pepper, and ginger, and sauté until onions are translucent.

3 | Add coriander, cumin, and turmeric, and cook for 1 minute. Add 2 tablespoons vegetable broth, potatoes, peas, and salt, and cook 2–3 more minutes. Set aside. Preheat oven to 400°F.

4 | After allowing pastry dough to rise for 45 minutes, roll out each ball to a diameter of 3 inches. Place 1½ heaping tablespoons of filling in the center. Fold pastry over and pinch edges together. There should be no openings along the edge.

5 | Bake at 400°F for 15–20 minutes.

SESAME NOODLE SALAD

PREPARATION TIME: 20 minutes

MAKES 4–6 SERVINGS

FOR THE SALAD
2 cups finely shredded green cabbage
1 red bell pepper, diced
2 medium carrots, shredded
1 cup peanuts, crushed
¼ cup sesame seeds
½ cup scallions, finely diced
4 ounces whole wheat pasta, cooked

FOR THE DRESSING
¼ cup light soy sauce
2 tablespoons tahini
1 tablespoon finely minced ginger
2 tablespoons balsamic vinegar
2 tablespoons agave
½ tablespoon Sambal Oelek
½ teaspoon black pepper

1 | Mix the cabbage, pepper, and carrots in a large salad bowl. Add peanuts, sesame seeds, scallions, and cooked pasta.

2 | Whisk together dressing ingredients. Pour over the salad. Toss to mix.

SOUTHWESTERN SALAD

PREPARATION TIME: 15 minutes

MAKES 8 SERVINGS

8 cups salad greens
1 small red onion, diced
1 green bell pepper, diced
2 tablespoons minced cilantro
¾ cup avocado, diced
3 medium tomatoes, diced
1 15-ounce can black beans, rinsed and drained
1 15-ounce can corn, drained
1 teaspoon oregano
½ teaspoon sea salt
1 cup baked tortilla chips, crushed

1 | Combine salad greens, onion, green pepper, cilantro, avocado, and tomatoes in a large salad bowl.

2 | Heat beans and corn for 4 minutes over medium heat. Add oregano and salt. Add to salad right before serving, together with tortilla chips.

3 | Sprinkle with rice vinegar, if desired.

TOMATO TORTILLA SOUP | 135

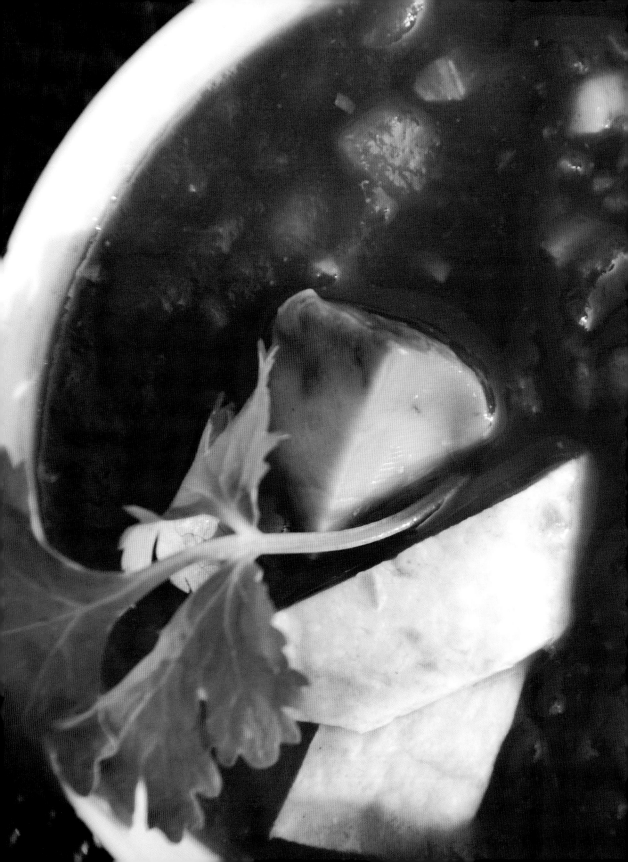

AZTEC SOUP

PREPARATION TIME: 20 minutes | COOKING TIME: 15 minutes

MAKES 4–6 SERVINGS

1 onion, chopped
4 cloves garlic, minced
¼ teaspoon cayenne pepper
1 tablespoon ground cumin
1 teaspoon smoked paprika
½ cup diced celery
3 cups vegetable broth, divided
2 15-ounce cans black beans,

drained and rinsed
1 cup frozen corn
3 tablespoons lime juice, divided
1 avocado, diced
1 tomato, diced
¼ cup chopped fresh cilantro
Sea salt and black pepper to taste

1 | Sauté onion and garlic in 2 tablespoons vegetable broth in a soup pot over medium-high heat, until onion is soft. Add seasonings and celery and cook for 1–2 minutes.

2 | Add vegetable broth, beans, corn, and 2 tablespoons lime juice. Bring to a boil, then reduce heat and simmer for 10 minutes. Season with salt and black pepper.

3 | In a separate bowl, combine avocado, tomato, cilantro, remaining 1 tablespoon lime juice, salt, and black pepper.

4 | Pour hot soup into bowls and top with a rounded tablespoon of avocado salsa.

TIPS

Try using frozen white corn or hominy for extra sweetness and flavor.

If you want a less spicy soup, only add a pinch of cayenne pepper.

This soup is also good served with tortilla chips.

COCONUT CORN CHOWDER

PREPARATION TIME: 20 minutes | COOKING TIME: 15 minutes
MAKES 6 SERVINGS 🍎 🌾 🥕 🌱

1 medium whole leek, cleaned and chopped
2 cloves garlic, minced
1 jalapeño pepper, chopped
4 small red potatoes, cleaned and thinly sliced
1 15-ounce can chickpeas, rinsed and drained
1 cup frozen corn
1 14-ounce can lite coconut milk
1½ cups vegetable broth, divided
½ teaspoon sea salt
¼ teaspoon red pepper flakes

1 | In a large soup pot, sauté leeks, garlic, jalapeño, and potatoes in ½ cup of vegetable broth over medium-high heat until vegetables are tender.

2 | Add chickpeas, corn, coconut milk, and remaining vegetable broth. Bring to a boil and simmer for 15 minutes until potatoes are tender and soup has thickened. Season with salt and pepper flakes.

3 | Serve hot.

TIPS

Slice and wash the leeks very carefully, as they have a tendency to be sandy.

If you prefer a thicker soup, add more vegetables and reduce the water.

DOMINICAN CHAPEA

PREPARATION TIME: 15 minutes | COOKING TIME: 35 minutes
MAKES 6–8 SERVINGS

6 cups vegetable broth, divided
1 medium onion, diced
4 cloves garlic, minced
¼ cup fresh cilantro, chopped
½ green bell pepper, diced
2 large carrots, sliced
1½ cups rice, uncooked

1 cup cabbage, chopped
1 can cooked pinto beans, rinsed
  and drained
1½ cups butternut squash, diced
4 tablespoons tomato paste
½ teaspoon sea salt (to taste)

1 | In large soup pot, add ¼ cup vegetable broth, onion, garlic, cilantro, and peppers. Cook over medium-high heat, stirring occasionally, until onions are translucent.

2 | Add remaining vegetable broth, carrots, rice, cabbage, pinto beans, squash, tomato paste, and salt. Bring to a boil. Stir regularly to prevent sticking.

3 | Once mixture comes to a boil, reduce temperature to low, cover, and cook for 30 minutes.

4 | This soup is done when the rice is fully cooked. Add more salt, if necessary.

TIPS

Serve topped with slices of avocados.

If you prefer a thinner soup, add 1–2 additional cups of vegetable broth.

GERMAN SAUERKRAUT SOUP

PREPARATION TIME: 15 minutes | COOKING TIME: 25 minutes
MAKES 4–6 SERVINGS

2 medium onions, diced
3 large carrots, chopped
3 celery ribs, chopped
4 cups vegetable broth, divided
2 cups sliced fresh mushrooms
2 cups potatoes, peeled and cubed
1 can vegan cream of mushroom soup
   (Amy's brand makes a vegan version)
1 14-ounce can sauerkraut
2 tablespoons white vinegar
2 teaspoons dried dill weed
1 teaspoon Sucanat
¼ teaspoon black pepper
Sea salt to taste

1 | Place onions, carrots, and celery in a large pot. Add ½ cup vegetable broth and cook until onions are translucent.

2 | Add remaining ingredients and simmer until potatoes are soft and tender.

HEARTY STEW

PREPARATION TIME: 30 minutes | COOKING TIME: 30 minutes
MAKES 4–6 SERVINGS 🍎 🌾 🥕 🫛

4 cups vegetable broth, divided
1 tablespoon soy sauce
1 onion, chopped
1 red bell pepper, diced
4 cloves garlic, minced
4 cups butternut or other winter squash
   (about 2 pounds), peeled, seeded,
   and cut into ½-inch cubes

1 medium potato, peeled and diced
2 15-ounce jars of your favorite
   salsa, medium-hot
1 tablespoon dried oregano
2 zucchinis, chopped
1 15-ounce can pinto beans
1½ cups corn
Sea salt to taste

1 | Heat ¼ cup vegetable broth and soy sauce in a large soup pot. Add onion, bell pepper, and garlic. Sauté over medium heat until the onion is soft.

2 | Add remaining vegetable broth, squash, and potatoes to the pot, along with the salsa and oregano. Cover and simmer until the squash is just tender when pierced with a fork, about 15 minutes.

3 | Add zucchini, pinto beans, and corn. Continue cooking another 10 minutes. Add salt to taste and serve hot.

TIPS

You can substitute white corn or hominy for the regular corn, for extra sweetness and flavor.

Canned beans can be replaced with dried beans that have been soaked and cooked.

Butternut squash is also available frozen.

LENTIL SOUP

PREPARATION TIME: 10 minutes | COOKING TIME: 45 minutes
MAKES 4–6 SERVINGS

1 onion, chopped
2 cloves garlic, minced
2 carrots, sliced
2 stalks celery, chopped
1 tablespoon curry powder
4½ cups vegetable broth, divided
1 cup brown lentils, rinsed

1 cup scallions, chopped
1 teaspoon lemon juice
1 tablespoon nutritional yeast
¼ teaspoon black pepper
¼ teaspoon red pepper flakes
Sea salt to taste

1 | In a large soup pot, sauté onion, garlic, carrots, and celery in ½ cup vegetable broth over medium-high heat, until vegetables are soft. Add curry powder and cook for 1 minute.

2 | Add remaining vegetable broth, lentils, scallions, lemon juice, nutritional yeast, black pepper, and red pepper flakes. Bring to a boil, then cover and turn heat low to a slow simmer, stirring occasionally, until the lentils are tender, about 45 minutes.

3 | Add salt to taste.

TIPS

Adding salt at the end of a recipe allows you to use just the right amount.

This soup can also be prepared in a Crock-Pot. If you start with boiling water, it will cook in 1–2 hours; with cold water, 5–6 hours.

You can prepare a pot of this delicious soup and keep it on hand for quick meals. Reheat individual portions in the microwave and serve it with a salad of mixed greens and a slice of whole grain bread for a thoroughly nutritious and satisfying meal.

THE HIGHER FIBER

There is a reason why we often hear that we need more fiber in our diet—our body needs fiber! A study in *The China Study* may give you that extra motivation you need to make a change in your diet. Whereas meat and animal protein consumption has been linked to higher rates of colon cancer, eating an "additional ten grams of dietary fiber a day lowered the long-term risk of colon cancer by 33%," which can be found in 1 cup of red raspberries, peas, or about any type of bean.* These plant based foods provide more than the necessary amount of fiber needed to fight off this disease, and can add flavor and variety to any dish.

The China Study, pg. 170

QUICK THREE-BEAN SOUP

PREPARATION TIME: 10 minutes | COOKING TIME: 35 minutes
MAKES 4–6 SERVINGS 🍅 🥕 🌶

2 tablespoons vegetable broth
1 medium onion, diced
4 cloves garlic, minced
1 15-ounce can black beans, rinsed and drained
1 15-ounce can red kidney beans, rinsed and drained
1 15-ounce can chickpeas, rinsed and drained
1 14-ounce can crushed tomatoes, with jalapeños
2 cups mixed vegetables (corn, green beans and/or carrots)
3 cups reduced-sodium vegetable broth
1 teaspoon smoked paprika
1 teaspoon black pepper
1 heaping teaspoon dried parsley
1 teaspoon oregano

1 | In a large soup pot, sauté onion and garlic in 2 tablespoons vegetable broth over medium-high heat until onion is slightly transparent.

2 | Add remaining ingredients. Cover and cook on medium-low heat for 30 minutes.

TIPS

For variety, leafy greens like kale or chard and seasonal vegetables like zucchini, carrots, green beans, and corn are especially good in this recipe as a substitution for the frozen vegetables.

This soup goes well with Fiesta Corn Bread (p. 44).

SEASONED MUSHROOM SOUP

PREPARATION TIME: 30 minutes | COOKING TIME: 21 minutes

MAKES 4 SERVINGS

2 tablespoons water
2 onions, chopped
1 cup vegetable broth
1 pound mushrooms, cleaned
 and sliced
1 tablespoon paprika
1 teaspoon dried dill

1 teaspoon caraway seeds (optional)
Black pepper to taste
3 tablespoons light soy sauce or tamari
2 tablespoons whole grain flour
2 cups soy milk, divided
1 tablespoon lemon juice
3 tablespoons red wine (optional)

1 | Heat 2 tablespoons water in a large soup pot and add onions. Cook over medium-high heat until onions are soft.

2 | Add vegetable broth, sliced mushrooms, paprika, dill, caraway seeds (if using), and black pepper. Lower the heat slightly and cook 5 minutes more, stirring frequently.

3 | Add soy sauce or tamari.

4 | In a separate pan, mix ¼ cup milk with flour to form a paste. Cook over medium heat, stirring constantly, for 1 minute. Then whisk in the remaining soy milk and cook until steamy and slightly thickened.

5 | Add the milk-flour mixture to the soup. Stir in the lemon juice (and wine, if using) just before serving.

SPICY PUMPKIN SOUP

PREPARATION TIME: 20 minutes | **COOKING TIME:** 25 minutes
MAKES 4 SERVINGS

½ medium onion, diced
2 tablespoons vegetable broth
1 teaspoon curry powder
1 teaspoon ground coriander
1 teaspoon ground cumin
½ teaspoon red pepper flakes
1 cup water
1 cup almond milk
1 medium potato, thinly sliced
1 15-ounce can pumpkin puree
Sea salt to taste

1 | In a large soup pot, sauté onion in vegetable broth over medium-high heat, until onion is tender.

2 | Stir in curry powder, cumin, coriander, and red pepper flakes. Reduce heat to low and cook for 1 additional minute.

3 | Add water, milk, potatoes, and pumpkin. Cook over medium heat for 10–15 minutes. Add salt to taste. Serve hot.

TIP

This is a fast, easy, delicious soup. If you prefer a smoother consistency, puree it with an immersion blender.

SEE PICTURE ON PAGE 117

TOMATO TORTILLA SOUP

PREPARATION TIME: 15 minutes | COOKING TIME: 17 minutes
MAKES 4 SERVINGS 🍎 🌾 🍃 🥕

¼ cup water
1 medium onion, diced
3–4 cloves garlic, minced
1 tablespoon minced jalapeño peppers
⅓ cup diced celery
¼ cup corn
1 28-ounce jar tomato sauce

2 cups vegetable broth
2 teaspoons Italian seasoning
2 tablespoons lime juice
6 small soft tortillas, cut into strips
Sea salt to taste
2 tablespoons chopped cilantro
1 avocado, diced

1 | In a large soup pot, sauté onion, garlic, jalapeño, and celery in ¼ cup water over medium-high heat until onions are soft.

2 | Stir in corn, tomato sauce, and vegetable broth. Bring to a boil, then reduce heat and simmer for 10 minutes.

3 | Add Italian seasoning, lime juice, and tortilla strips. Simmer for 2 minutes.

4 | Season with salt. Serve garnished with cilantro and avocado.

TIPS

If you like a stronger cilantro taste, add ¼ cup of cilantro.

If you want a heartier soup, add 1 cup diced sweet potatoes in step 1.

THAI PEANUT SOUP

PREPARATION TIME: 15 minutes | COOKING TIME: 20 minutes
MAKES 4–6 SERVINGS

4 tablespoons vegetable broth
3 scallions, diced (green and white)
1 stalk celery, diced
1 large carrot, diced
½ red bell pepper, seeded and diced
1 jalapeño pepper, minced
2 tablespoons fresh ginger, diced
1 medium head broccoli, chopped
½ tablespoon finely chopped
  lemongrass, white portion only

¾ cup water
1 15-ounce can unsweetened coconut
  milk
⅓ cup natural peanut butter
2 tablespoons tamari or light
  soy sauce
1 teaspoon Sambal Oelek (Chili paste)
Sea salt and black pepper to taste

1 | In a large soup pot, add vegetable broth and sauté scallions, celery, carrot, red pepper, jalapeño pepper, ginger, broccoli, and lemongrass over medium-high heat until vegetables are soft.

2 | Add water, coconut milk, peanut butter, and tamari or soy sauce. Reduce heat to medium and stir until well combined. Cook about 15 minutes.

3 | Add Sambal Oelek and season with salt and pepper.

TIP

Sambal Oelek is an Asian chili paste and can be found in most Asian and world markets; if your local grocery store has a good international section, it will most likely carry Sambal Oelek.

SANDWICHES

SEE PICTURE ON PAGE 139

VEGGIE SUBS

PREPARATION TIME: 15 minutes

MAKES 6 SUBS 🍎 🌾 🍃 🥕

6 whole grain submarine buns
Green Garden Mayonnaise (p. 108)
1 large cucumber, sliced
1 large tomato, sliced
1 green bell pepper, seeded and sliced
1 red bell pepper, seeded and sliced
1 cup shredded carrot
2 cups leaf lettuce and/or raw spinach

1 large red onion, thinly sliced
1 large avocado, cut into slices or wedges
Sliced pickles
1 cup sliced black olives (optional)
⅓ cup red wine vinegar
Oregano (optional)
Sea salt and black pepper to taste

1 | Slice the buns almost all the way through. Heat them briefly in a low-heat oven or toaster oven.

2 | Spread mayonnaise on bun. Layer cucumber, tomato, peppers, carrot, lettuce, onion, avocado, pickles, and olives on top of mayonnaise. Drizzle with red wine vinegar. Add oregano (if using) and a bit of salt and pepper.

3 | Close sandwich and serve immediately.

TIPS

You can also cut all the ingredients and place them on a plate. This allows each person to pick and choose his or her favorite combination.

To add some heat, use diced jalapeños.

DELICIOUS EGGLESS SANDWICHES

PREPARATION TIME: 10 minutes

MAKES 6 SANDWICHES 🍎 🌾 🍃 🥕 🫛

12 ounces extra-firm tofu, drained
  and mashed
4 tablespoons red onion, finely diced
4 tablespoons Green Garden
  Mayonnaise (p. 108)
4 tablespoons dill pickle, diced
1 celery stalk, diced
1 medium carrot, finely grated in
  food processor

2 tablespoons rice vinegar
1 teaspoon ground mustard
1 teaspoon turmeric
½ teaspoon sea salt
8 slices whole wheat bread
4 leaves lettuce
4 slices tomato

1 | Combine tofu with onion, mayonnaise, pickle, celery, carrot, rice vinegar, mustard, turmeric, and salt in a large mixing bowl. Mix thoroughly.

2 | Spread on whole wheat bread, and top with lettuce and tomato slices.

TIPS

Make sure you're actually getting whole wheat bread by reading the ingredient list: the first ingredient listed should be whole wheat flour.

Tofu varies greatly in flavor and texture, so sample several brands to find your favorite. Natural foods stores usually have a wider selection of tofu than supermarkets do. The freshest tofu has the best taste. Be sure to select fresh tofu by checking the expiration date on the package.

Mayonnaise is generally made with eggs and oil and is rich in fat, animal protein, and cholesterol. When purchasing premade mayonnaise, choose a soy mayonnaise that is not made with eggs, and read the labels to find one that is low in fat.

SPINACHE CHICKPEA BURGERS

PREPARATION TIME: 20 minutes | COOKING TIME: 50 minutes

MAKES 6–8 BURGERS, DEPENDING ON THICKNESS

¼ cup water
2 tablespoons flaxseed meal
2 tablespoons vegetable broth
½ small onion, peeled and chopped
1 large carrot, chopped
1 cup packed frozen spinach
1 tablespoon tomato paste
1 15-ounce can garbanzo beans
    (chickpeas), drained
½ teaspoon paprika

1 teaspoon cumin
1 teaspoon coriander
½ tablespoon garlic powder
1 tablespoon vital wheat gluten
1 cup old-fashioned rolled oats (not
    quick-cooking)
Sea salt and black pepper to taste
8 ounce Panko style bread crumbs
6–8 whole grain burger buns
Your favorite burger toppings

1 | Combine flaxseed meal and water. Set aside for 5–10 minutes.

2 | Sauté onions, carrots, and spinach in vegetable broth. Once tender place in food processor. Add tomato paste and garbanzo beans and pulse 5–8 times until mixture resembles burger crumbles. (Do not make paste.)

3 | Pour ingredients into bowl with flaxseed meal and water. Stir in spices, vital wheat gluten, and oats. Season with salt and pepper. Form patties ¼–½" in thickness.

4 | Preheat oven to 350°F. Spread bread crumbs on a plate. Turn the burgers in the bread crumbs so that they are coated on all sides.

5 | Place coated patties on parchment-covered baking sheet. Bake for 25 minutes on each side until burgers are firm but not dried out.

6 | Serve on a whole wheat bun with your favorite toppings.

GRANOLA FRUIT WRAPS

PREPARATION TIME: 10 minutes | 🍎 🌾 🫛

Large flour tortillas (or other whole grain sandwich wraps)
Natural peanut butter
Low-fat granola
Grapes
Apples, peeled and diced

1 | Place tortilla in the microwave and heat for about 15 seconds.

2 | Spread peanut butter down the middle of the tortilla in a 2-inch strip. Do not cover the entire tortilla.

3 | Place two handfuls of granola on top of the peanut butter.

4 | Place two medium handfuls of grapes on top of granola.

5 | Placed diced apples on top of grapes.

6 | Fold the tortilla, first from the bottom and then from the sides, like a burrito.

TIP

This recipe makes the perfect almost-instant snack! My sons absolutely love this wrap. During the summer, when there are fresh blueberries, they replace the grapes with blueberries.

HUMMUS WRAPS

PREPARATION TIME: 10 minutes

MAKES 6–10 WRAPS

¼ cup water
1 15-ounce can chickpeas, rinsed and drained
2 cloves garlic, minced
¼ cup tahini
2 tablespoons freshly squeezed lemon juice
Sea salt, paprika, and cumin to taste
6–10 large tortillas
Lettuce and tomato

1 | Combine water, chickpeas, garlic, tahini, freshly squeezed lemon juice, sea salt, paprika, and cumin in the bowl of a food processor. Blend thoroughly.

2 | Spread on tortillas and top with lettuce and tomato slices.

TIP

You can flavor hummus by adding your favorite vegetable or spice, such as roasted red peppers, horseradish, extra garlic, cayenne pepper, or sun-dried tomatoes.

OCEAN CHICKPEA SANDWICHES

PREPARATION TIME: 10 minutes

MAKES 8 SANDWICHES

1 can chickpeas, drained and rinsed
5 tablespoons Green Garden Mayonnaise (p. 108)
1 tablespoon mustard
4 tablespoons diced dill pickle
4 tablespoons finely diced onion
1 celery stalk, diced
2 tablespoons rice vinegar
½ teaspoon kelp powder
Sea salt and black pepper to taste
8 slices whole wheat bread
4 leaves lettuce
4 slices tomato

1 | Place chickpeas in food processor and pulse two times to roughly chop. Add mayonnaise, mustard, pickle, onion, celery, rice vinegar, kelp powder, salt, and pepper. Mix thoroughly.

2 | Spread on whole wheat bread and top with lettuce and tomato slices.

TIP

Kelp powder is found in health food stores and adds a great "seafood" taste to this dish.

PECAN BALL SUBS

PREPARATION TIME: 15 minutes | BAKING TIME: 40–45 minutes
MAKES 6 SANDWICHES

1 14-ounce package extra-firm tofu
½ cup pecans
½ cup chopped onion
½ cup chopped carrot
2 cloves garlic
¼ cup fresh parsley
1 teaspoon dried thyme
2 tablespoons nutritional yeast
1 teaspoon salt

1 teaspoon dried basil
1 tablespoon light soy sauce
1 tablespoon lemon juice
1 cup bread crumbs
1 cup raw oats
1 recipe Marinara Sauce (p. 191) or your
   favorite spaghetti sauce
6 whole wheat submarine sandwich buns

1 | Preheat oven to 350°F.

2 | In food processor, blend tofu, pecans, onion, carrot, garlic, parsley, thyme, nutritional yeast, salt, basil, soy sauce, and lemon juice. Place mixture in a large mixing bowl.

3 | Mix in bread crumbs and oats.

4 | Roll into balls about 2 inches in diameter and place on a baking sheet lined with parchment paper.

5 | Bake for 40–45 minutes.

6 | Place pecan balls in sandwich buns and top with marinara sauce.

TIP

These make great mock "meatballs" for spaghetti and tomato sauce.

PORTOBELLO THYME SANDWICHES

PREPARATION TIME: 8 minutes | COOKING TIME: 10 minutes
MAKES 4 SANDWICHES 🍎 🌾 🍐 🌿 🍄

Portobello mushrooms have a unique flavor and are considered the "steak" of the vegan world.

FOR THE DRESSING
2 cloves garlic, minced or pressed
½ cup balsamic vinegar
1 teaspoon dried thyme
2 tablespoons agave
Sea salt and black pepper to taste

FOR THE SANDWICHES
4 large portobello mushroom caps (or cut
   baby portobellos)
4 whole wheat sandwich buns
¼ cup Green Garden Mayonnaise (p. 108)
4 leaves lettuce
1 large tomato, sliced
1 medium red onion, thinly sliced

1 | In a shallow bowl, make the dressing by whisking garlic, vinegar, thyme, agave, and salt and pepper.

2 | Place the mushroom cap-side down in dressing mixture and marinate for 1 hour.

3 | Turn on broiler and adjust rack so it is close to the heat source.

4 | Put the caps under the broiler and cook for 5 minutes. Turn the caps over and broil for 4 more minutes. Toast the buns lightly.

5 | Spread mayonnaise mixture on the buns. Place mushroom caps on the buns and top with lettuce, tomato, and red onion.

TASTY TOSTADOS

PREPARATION TIME: 15 minutes
MAKES 4 SERVINGS 🍎 🌾 🍃 🌶

---

1 15-ounce can pinto beans, rinsed and drained *Also 1 can refried beans*
4 thick gordita-style tortillas, heated *- make large pitas*
½ cup cabbage, finely grated *opt.*
1 avocado, diced *- mash with lemon juice + sea salt*
½ cup low-sodium salsa (you pick the heat)

1 | Blend pinto beans in a food processor until smooth.

2 | Heat beans in a skillet over medium heat for 5–6 minutes.

3 | Heat a tortilla in an ungreased skillet until it is warm and soft. Spread bean mixture over the tortilla. Top with cabbage, avocado, and salsa.

TIPS

Be sure to select a tortilla made without lard.

Nonfat refried beans can be used in place of pinto beans.

Top with fresh cilantro, if desired.

Additional toppings that go well on this dish are chopped onions, fresh tomatoes, and olives.

Layer avocado pulp under beans + salsa on top.

Very Good

THAI WRAPS

PREPARATION TIME: 15 minutes
MAKES 4 WRAPS

This is a surprisingly tasty recipe. My sons and friends love these wraps.

1 12.3-ounce package extra-firm tofu
⅓ cup peanut butter
4 tablespoons light soy sauce
1 tablespoon lime juice
⅛ teaspoon garlic powder
⅛ teaspoon cayenne pepper
¼ cup red bell pepper, chopped
¼ cup red onion, finely chopped
½ cup grated carrot
1 stalk celery, finely chopped
¼ cup chopped cilantro
¼ teaspoon powdered ginger
4 10-inch whole grain tortillas, or 8 slices
    whole grain bread, or 4 pita pockets
4 leaves leaf lettuce

1 | Drain tofu. Place in medium bowl and crumble with a fork.

2 | Add peanut butter, soy sauce, lime juice, garlic powder, cayenne pepper, bell pepper, onion, carrot, celery, cilantro, and powdered ginger. Stir with a fork until well mixed.

3 | Top tortillas with lettuce and then spread tofu mixture evenly over each lettuce leaf. Fold wrap like a burrito.

TOMATO BASIL PESTO SANDWICHES

PREPARATION TIME: 10 minutes

MAKES 4 SANDWICHES

2 cups fresh basil leaves, packed
½ cup pine nuts
3 medium-sized garlic cloves, minced
⅓ cup water
Sea salt and black pepper to taste
8 slices of whole grain bread
2 large tomatoes, sliced

1 | To make pesto, combine basil with pine nuts in a food processor. Pulse a few times. Add garlic and pulse a few more times.

2 | Slowly add water while the food processor is on. Add salt and pepper.

3 | Toast bread and spread with pesto. Add sliced tomatoes and enjoy.

VEGGIE FAJITA WRAPS

PREPARATION TIME: 25 minutes | COOKING TIME: 5 minutes

MAKES 8 SERVINGS 🍎 🌾 🍃 🥕 🌻 🍄

½ cup vegetable broth, divided
2 cloves garlic, minced
½ onion, sliced
2 green bell peppers, seeded and sliced
2 yellow, red or orange bell peppers,
    seeded and sliced
2 large carrots, cut into thin strips
1 head broccoli, cut into florets
1 cup sliced mushrooms

3 green onions, chopped
1 tablespoon green chilies
Lemon pepper and sea salt to taste
12 whole grain flour tortillas
1 large tomato, diced
2 cups shredded lettuce
1 large avocado, sliced
Salsa or favorite non-fat dressing

1 | In a large, nonstick skillet over medium-high heat, sauté garlic and onion in 2 tablespoons vegetable broth. Add peppers, carrots, broccoli, and additional ¼ cup vegetable broth. Cover and cook on medium heat for 2 minutes. Add mushrooms, green onions, chilies, and additional 2 tablespoons vegetable broth. Re-cover and cook for 1 additional minute.

2 | Season the vegetables with lemon pepper and salt. Stir well.

3 | Assemble fajita: place a small amount of cooked vegetables in the center of your tortilla along with diced tomatoes, lettuce, avocado, and salsa. Roll and enjoy.

TIPS

Lemon pepper can be purchased with or without salt. Make sure you buy the variety without salt; then, if you desire, add the salt to your fajita separately.

You can substitute or add more vegetables to this recipe, depending on the season. Zucchini and yellow squash make good summertime additions.

ENTRÉES

AFRICAN VEGETABLES

PREPARATION TIME: 15 minutes | **COOKING TIME:** 20–25 minutes

MAKES 6–8 SERVINGS

2 tablespoons vegetable broth
1 medium onion, chopped
1 green bell pepper, chopped
4 cloves garlic, minced
¼ teaspoon cayenne pepper
1 teaspoon cinnamon
1 cup water
1 large sweet potato, peeled and
  cut into 1-inch cubes

2 cups frozen chopped spinach
½ cup frozen corn
4 tablespoons tomato paste
1 15-ounce can diced tomatoes
1 medium zucchini, peeled and sliced
¼ cup natural peanut butter
Sea salt and black pepper to taste
2 cups cooked brown rice, for serving

1 | In large soup pot, add 2 tablespoons of vegetable broth, onion, pepper, and garlic. Cook over medium-high heat until onion and pepper are soft.

2 | Reduce heat to medium. Add cayenne pepper and cinnamon. Cook 1–2 minutes longer.

3 | Add water, sweet potato, spinach, corn, tomato paste, diced tomatoes, and zucchini. Bring the mixture to a boil, reduce heat, cover, and simmer for 10 minutes or until potato is easily pricked with a fork. If necessary, add more water.

4 | Stir in peanut butter, salt, and pepper. Cook over medium heat for 5 more minutes.

5 | Serve over cooked rice.

ASPARAGUS CREPES

PREPARATION TIME: 15 minutes | COOKING TIME: 15 minutes
BAKING TIME: 15 minutes | MAKES 6 CREPES 🌾 🍃 🐚

FOR THE CREPES
1 cup whole wheat pastry flour
2 egg replacers (2 tablespoons
    ground flaxseed meal with
    6 tablespoons water)
1½–2 cups plain nondairy milk

FOR THE FILLING
¼ cup vegetable broth
3 cups chopped asparagus, cut
    into bite-sized pieces
3 cloves garlic, pressed
2 tablespoons lemon juice

¼ teaspoon dried tarragon
1 teaspoon onion powder
½ teaspoon sea salt

FOR THE SAUCE
4 tablespoons Green Garden
    Mayonnaise (p. 108)
2 tablespoons lemon juice
1 tablespoon nutritional yeast
½ teaspoon salt
pinch red pepper flakes
2 tablespoons nondairy milk

1 | For crepes, combine flour and egg replacers in a medium bowl. Slowly stir in the milk and beat with a wire whisk until the batter is smooth.

2 | Pour ¼ cup batter in nonstick skillet or crepe pan. Tilt and rotate the skillet to distribute the batter evenly over the bottom of the pan. Cook for 1 minute or until bubbles appear on surface of crepe. Turn the crepe over and cook briefly on the other side. Repeat this process with the remaining batter.

3 | Preheat oven to 350°F.

4 | For the filling, sauté asparagus in ¼ cup vegetable broth in a large skillet over medium-high heat until tender.

5 | Add garlic, lemon juice, tarragon, onion powder, and salt. Sauté for 1 minute more. Set aside.

6 | To assemble, place asparagus in center of crepe. Roll up and place in a large baking dish.

7 | Cover and bake for 15 minutes. While crepes are baking, whisk together sauce ingredients, and after crepes are baked, spread the sauce over the top of each crepe. Serve immediately.

BAKED STUFFED TOMATOES WITH COUSCOUS

PREPARATION TIME: 15 minutes | COOKING TIME: 15 minutes
BAKING TIME: 15–20 minutes | MAKES 6–8 SERVINGS

8 large steak tomatoes (firm ones are best)
3 cups whole wheat couscous, cooked
    according to package directions
4 tablespoons vegetable broth, divided
1 medium onion, diced
2 cloves garlic, diced
½ cup fresh basil, chopped
½ cup pine nuts

2 tablespoons nutritional yeast
1 teaspoon paprika
1½ cups frozen spinach leaves
Sea salt and black pepper to taste
1 tablespoon balsamic vinegar
    (per person/optional)

1 | Preheat oven to 350°F.

2 | Cut the tomatoes in half and scoop out the insides. Turn the tomatoes upside down to drain while you prepare the stuffing.

3 | Cook the couscous according to package directions. Set aside.

4 | Place onion and garlic in a large skillet with 2 tablespoons vegetable broth and cook over medium-high heat.

5 | Add basil, pine nuts, nutritional yeast, paprika, and spinach with 2 more tablespoons of vegetable broth. Cook for 1–2 minutes until spinach is cooked. Remove from heat.

6 | Stir in couscous and season with salt and pepper.

7 | Spoon the couscous mixture into the tomatoes and place in an 8 × 8 baking dish. If there is additional couscous, place in baking dish around the tomatoes.

8 | Bake uncovered for 15–20 minutes. Serve hot. Drizzle with balsamic vinegar.

BURGER SALAD

PREPARATION TIME: 25 minutes
MAKES 4 SERVINGS

This recipe is adapted from a dish that we often ordered from one of my parents' favorite restaurants in Ithaca, New York, ABC Café—which is no longer in operation.

FOR THE DRESSING
¼ cup lite soy sauce
2 tablespoons tahini
1 tablespoon ginger, minced
½ cup balsamic vinegar
2 tablespoons agave
½ tablespoon Sambal Oelek

FOR THE SALAD
2 cups shredded lettuce
½ cup shredded purple cabbage
2 large carrots, shredded

1 large cucumber, diced
1 green bell pepper, seeded and cut in
  ½-inch chunks
½ red bell pepper, seeded and cut in
  ½-inch chunks
1 large tomato, cut in ½-inch chunks

OTHER INGREDIENTS
2 cups cooked brown rice
4 Spinache Chickpea Burgers (p. 143)
  or your favorite vegan burgers

1 | For dressing, whisk together all ingredients. Store in refrigerator until ready to use.

2 | Combine salad ingredients in a large mixing bowl. Toss to combine.

3 | Heap each serving dish with salad. In the center, place 3 heaping tablespoons of rice and 1 burger. Sprinkle with dressing.

4 | Serve immediately.

DOMINICAN BEANS

PREPARATION TIME: 15 minutes | **COOKING TIME:** 35 minutes

MAKES 6–8 SERVINGS

What really makes this dish is the salad served on top. The crunchy freshness of the vegetables and the tanginess of the dressing make for a perfect combination.

FOR THE BEANS
¼ cup vegetable broth, divided
1 onion, diced
4 cloves garlic, minced or pressed
1 medium green bell pepper, diced
½ cup diced butternut squash
½ cup chopped cilantro
1 cup water
3 tablespoons tomato paste
2 cans pinto beans
½ tablespoon Mexican oregano
   leaves, dried
½ teaspoon thyme, dried

Sea salt to taste
4 cups cooked brown rice, for serving

FOR THE SALAD
2 cups sliced lettuce
2 cups cabbage, sliced into strips
¾ cup sliced cucumber
¾ cup sliced cooked beets
1 tomato, sliced
1 large avocado, sliced
Balsamic rice vinegar
¼ teaspoon salt
¼ teaspoon pepper

1 | For the beans, heat 2 tablespoons vegetable broth in a large stock pot and sauté the onion and garlic over medium-high heat until soft. Add green pepper, squash, cilantro, and two more tablespoons vegetable broth. Cook for 2 minutes, stirring.

2 | Add water, tomato paste, beans, oregano, and thyme. Bring to a simmer and cook, uncovered, for 15 minutes. If needed, add an additional ½ cup water. Season with salt.

3 | While the beans are cooking, make the salad. In a large mixing bowl, combine all ingredients.

4 | Serve beans over rice and top with salad.

TIP

Black or red beans can be substituted for the pinto beans.

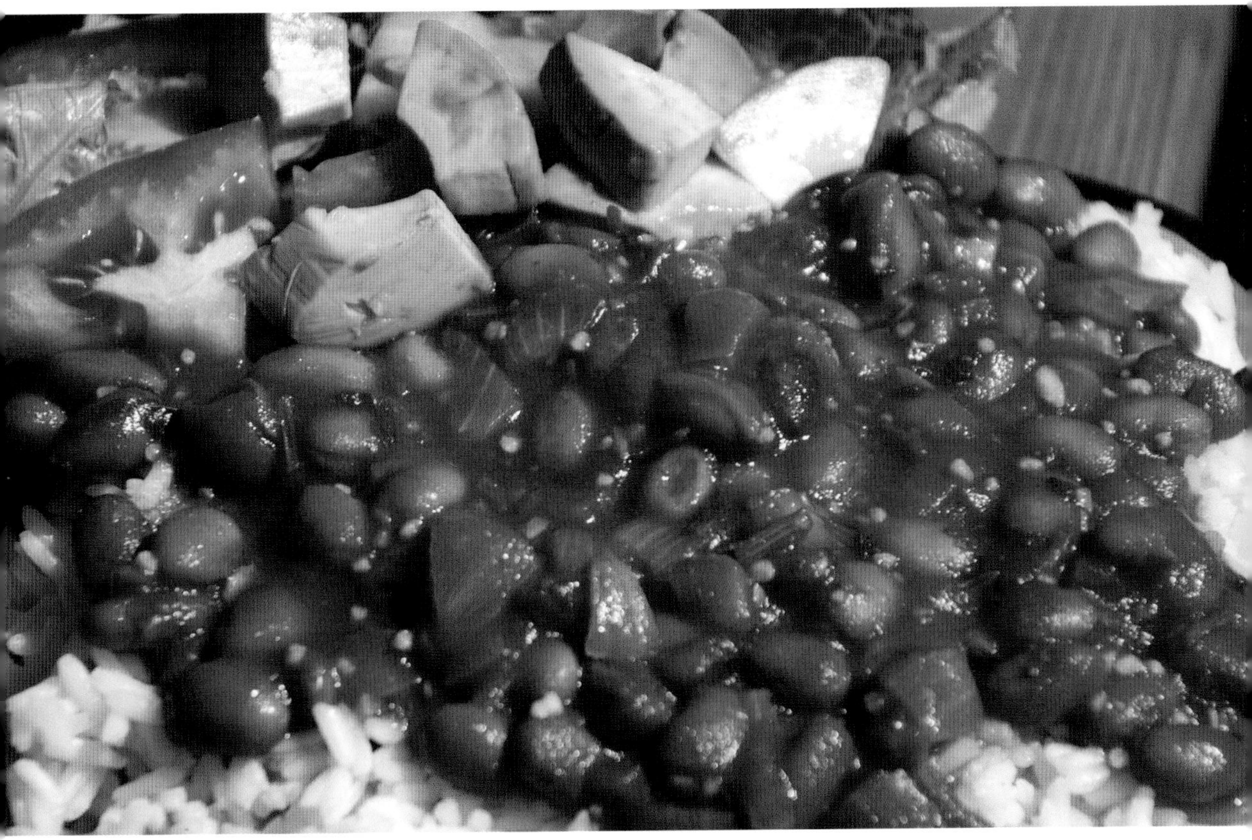

ZESTY BULGUR STEW

PREPARATION TIME: 10 minutes | COOKING TIME: 40 minutes
MAKES 4–6 SERVINGS 🍎 🌾 🥕 🌱

6 cups vegetable broth, divided
2 cloves garlic
1 medium onion, diced
1 15-ounce can chickpeas, drained and rinsed
½ cup bulgur
½ cup yellow lentils
1½ cups sweet potatoes, diced
½ teaspoon cayenne pepper
1 teaspoon sea salt
1 tablespoon ground coriander

1 | Sauté garlic and onions in 2 tablespoons vegetable broth.

2 | Add remaining vegetable broth, chickpeas, bulgur, and lentils in a soup pot. Bring to a boil, then simmer, partially covered, for 15 minutes.

3 | Add sweet potatoes and seasonings. Continue to cook for 25 minutes, or until sweet potatoes and lentils are tender.

4 | Serve immediately.

COCONUT CURRY RICE

PREPARATION TIME: 10 minutes | **COOKING TIME:** 30–35 minutes
MAKES 6 SERVINGS 🍎 🌾 🍃 🌶

2 tablespoons vegetable broth
1 medium onion, diced
1 large green bell pepper, diced
2 tablespoons minced garlic
2 teaspoons ground cumin
1 15-ounce can pinto beans, drained
   and rinsed

4 cups water
1 13.5-ounce can unsweetened lite
   coconut milk
6 ounces fresh spinach or 1 packet
   frozen spinach, thawed and drained
2 cups uncooked brown rice
Sea salt to taste

1 | Heat 2 tablespoons vegetable broth in a large pot and cook the onion, pepper, and garlic over medium-high heat until vegetables are soft. Add cumin and beans.

2 | Add water, coconut milk, spinach, and rice. Bring to a boil. Then reduce heat to low, cover, and cook for 30–35 minutes, stirring every 7–10 minutes until rice is cooked.

3 | Season with salt. Serve hot.

EGGPLANT BAKE

PREPARATION TIME: 20 minutes | **BAKING TIME:** 50 minutes
MAKES 6 SERVINGS

½ cup whole grain pastry flour
½–¾ cups soy milk
1–2 cups Italian bread crumbs
1 large eggplant, peeled, sliced ¼- to ½-inch thick, lengthwise
2 28-ounce jars of marinara sauce (or a double batch of Marinara Sauce, p. 191)
1 10-ounce package spaghetti or other whole grain long noodles, cooked

1 | Preheat oven to 350°F.

2 | Place pastry flour in a shallow bowl. Pour milk in a second shallow bowl. Place bread crumbs in a third shallow bowl. Bread eggplant slices by first dredging each slice in the flour, then covering with milk, and finally covering with bread crumbs. You may need to add more flour, milk, or bread crumbs depending on the number of slices your eggplant yields.

3 | Place breaded slices on a parchment-lined baking sheet. Bake for 20 minutes, until brown, turning once halfway through. Remove from oven, but keep oven at 350°F.

4 | Spread ½ cup marinara sauce over bottom of a 3-quart baking dish. Layer with eggplant slices. Add another layer of marinara. Top with remaining eggplant slices and cover with marinara sauce.

5 | Cover with foil and bake for 30 minutes. Serve on top of spaghetti.

SEE PICTURE ON PAGE 161

PORTOBELLOS WITH SPINACH

PREPARATION TIME: 25 minutes | **BAKING TIME:** 25–30 minutes

MAKES 6 SERVINGS

30 baby portobello mushrooms
¼ cup vegetable broth
½ large onion, diced
4 cloves garlic, minced
1 stalk celery, diced
1 teaspoon thyme, dried
1 teaspoon Worcestershire sauce
4 tablespoons red wine
½ teaspoon salt
¼ teaspoon black pepper
1 cup bread crumbs
12 cups fresh spinach, steamed until wilted, then drained

1 | Clean the mushrooms and remove the stems.

2 | Heat 2 tablespoons vegetable broth in a medium skillet over medium-high heat. Add onion, garlic, and celery and cook until onions are soft. Remove from heat.

3 | Stir in remaining 2 tablespoons vegetable broth, thyme, Worcestershire sauce, salt, black pepper, red wine, and bread crumbs. Mixture should stick together. If not, add additional vegetable broth.

4 | Stuff mushrooms with filling. Place stuffed mushrooms in nonstick baking dish. Bake, covered at 350° for 25–30 minutes.

5 | Meanwhile place steamed spinach on a serving platter and top with cooked mushrooms.

6 | Serve immediately.

FABULOUS SWEET POTATO ENCHILADAS

PREPARATION TIME: 20 minutes | BAKING TIME: 25 minutes

MAKES 6–8 SERVINGS

½ cup vegetable broth, divided
1 medium onion, diced
5 cloves garlic, minced
1 teaspoon coriander
2 teaspoons ground cumin
2 cups fresh spinach, chopped

2 cups black beans, chopped in a food processor
4 tablespoons soy sauce
3 cups cooked, mashed sweet potatoes
Sea salt, to taste
10 large tortillas
1 jar of your favorite salsa

1 | Preheat oven to 350°F.

2 | Heat 2 tablespoons vegetable broth in a medium skillet over medium-high heat. Add onion and garlic. Sauté until onion is translucent. Add coriander and cumin. Cook for 1 minute, stirring constantly.

3 | Add remaining vegetable broth, spinach, black beans, soy sauce, and mashed sweet potatoes. Cook for 3–5 minutes. Remove from heat and season with salt.

4 | Place ¼–½ cup of mixture in center of tortilla. Roll into a burrito and place in a nonstick baking dish.

5 | Once all the burritos are assembled, pour your favorite salsa on top and cover with aluminum foil.

6 | Bake for 25 minutes.

FAVORITE CHILI WITH PASTA

PREPARATION TIME: 15 minutes | **COOKING TIME:** 20 minutes
MAKES 6–8 SERVINGS

8 ounces whole wheat (or rice or vegetable) pasta spirals
¼ cup vegetable broth, divided
1 onion, chopped
3 cloves garlic, minced
2 tablespoons oregano
1 tablespoon chili powder
¼ teaspoon cayenne pepper

1 small green bell pepper, diced
1 large carrot, grated
1 15-ounce can diced tomatoes with jalapeños
2 15-ounce cans kidney beans
1 15-ounce package frozen corn
Sea salt to taste

1 | Cook pasta in boiling water until tender. Drain and rinse under hot water, then set aside.

2 | Heat 2 tablespoons vegetable broth in a large pot. Add onion, garlic, oregano, chili powder, and cayenne. Cook until onion is soft.

3 | Add 2 tablespoons vegetable broth, green pepper, carrots, diced tomatoes, kidney beans, and corn. Simmer over medium heat, stirring occasionally, for 10 minutes. Season with salt.

4 | Serve on top of cooked pasta.

FETTUCCINE WITH BROCCOLI AND CASHEW SAUCE

PREPARATION TIME: 15 minutes | **COOKING TIME:** 20 minutes
MAKES 6 SERVINGS 🌾 🌻 🌰

6 cups broccoli, chopped
8 ounces whole wheat fettuccine
½ cup raw cashews
1–1½ cups water
2 tablespoons vegetable broth
6 large cloves garlic, minced
1 tablespoon miso
½ tablespoon nutritional yeast
1 teaspoon tahini
¼ teaspoon smoked paprika
Salt and pepper to taste

1 | Steam broccoli over boiling water until it is just tender, about 5 minutes. It should be bright green and still slightly crisp. Drain and set aside.

2 | Cook fettuccine in boiling water until it is just tender. Drain and rinse quickly.

3 | Process cashews and water in blender until smooth.

4 | Heat 2 tablespoons vegetable broth in a skillet over medium-high heat. Sauté the garlic. Add cashews mixture, miso, nutritional yeast, tahini, and smoked paprika. Cook over medium heat for 7 minutes. Season with salt and pepper.

5 | Spread the fettuccine on a large platter, top with broccoli, and add sauce. Serve hot.

TIPS

Be sure to use the broccoli stems, trimmed. They are crunchy and delicious.

For a cheesier flavor, add 2–4 tablespoons of nutritional yeast to cashew sauce.

For extra flavor, use tomato basil fettuccine or try a wheatless fettuccine such as artichoke or corn.

CORN AND TOMATILLO STEW

PREPARATION TIME: 15 minutes | **COOKING TIME:** 25 minutes
MAKES 6–8 SERVINGS

---

1 large onion, chopped
3 cloves garlic, minced
4 cups vegetable broth, divided
6 ears of corn, shaved (about 6 cups kernels)
1 large potato, diced
2 ½ cups tomatillos, husked and chopped
1 jalapeño pepper, seeded and coarsely chopped
¼ cup chopped cilantro
½ teaspoon onion powder
½ teaspoon oregano
1 teaspoon paprika
Sea salt to taste

1 | In a soup pot, sauté onion and garlic in 2 tablespoons vegetable broth over medium heat, stirring frequently. Cook for 1–3 minutes, until garlic is fragrant.

2 | Add remaining vegetable broth, corn, and potato. Bring to a boil, then reduce heat and simmer for 10–15 minutes until potato and corn are cooked. Potatoes are done when they are easily pierced with a fork.

3 | Add tomatillos and jalapeño pepper. Cook about 5 minutes, until tomatillos are tender.

4 | Add cilantro, onion powder, oregano, and paprika, and season with salt. Simmer for 5 more minutes.

5 | Serve as is or on top of rice.

TIPS

Tomatillos can be bought in most grocery stores; they add a wonderful flavor.

The final consistency of this recipe should be thicker than a soup, more like a stew.

LEAFY LENTILS

PREPARATION TIME: 15 minutes | **COOKING TIME:** 35–40 minutes
MAKES 4–6 SERVINGS

1 cup uncooked lentils
2–3 cups vegetable broth
1 large onion, diced
1 tablespoon minced garlic
3 tablespoons dried oregano
2 cups diced tomatoes with jalapeños
4 tablespoons tomato paste
14 ounces chopped spinach, fresh or frozen
1 tablespoon balsamic vinegar
Sea salt and black pepper to taste
4 cups cooked brown rice, for serving

1 | Place lentils in a large saucepan with 2 cups vegetable broth. Bring to a boil over medium heat, then reduce heat and simmer for 25–30 minutes until lentils are tender. If needed, add more vegetable broth. When lentils are cooked, drain and set aside.

2 | In a large saucepan, sauté onion in 2 tablespoons of vegetable broth over medium heat, until softened. Add garlic, oregano, tomatoes, tomato paste, and cooked lentils, and cook for 4–5 minutes. Add spinach. Cover and cook until spinach is wilted, 3–4 minutes.

3 | Add vinegar and season with salt and pepper. Serve hot over a bed of brown rice.

LEEK PIE

PREPARATION TIME: 25 minutes | COOKING/BAKING TIME: 50 minutes–1 hour

MAKES 6 SERVINGS

FOR THE CRUST
2 medium potatoes, grated
6 ounces silken tofu
¼ cup soy milk
2 tablespoons nutritional yeast
2 tablespoons almond meal
¼ teaspoon nutmeg
¼ teaspoon sea salt
¼ teaspoon black pepper

FOR THE FILLING
2 tablespoons vegetable broth
3 medium leeks, chopped
   (about 4 cups)

3 cloves garlic, minced
2 tablespoons white wine
6 ounces silken tofu, drained and crumbled
1 tablespoon lemon juice
1 teaspoon sea salt
1 cup whole wheat bread crumbs
1 teaspoon tarragon, dried
1 tablespoon thyme, dried
1 cup sliced mushrooms
½ cup chopped sun-dried tomatoes (avoid
   the kind packed in oil)
½ cup soy milk
1 can of chopped black olives (optional)

1 | For the crust, preheat oven to 350°F. Wash and grate potatoes. Squeeze grated potatoes and drain moisture from them. Stir in tofu, milk, nutritional yeast, almond meal, nutmeg, salt, and pepper.

2 | Spread and pat potatoes into nonstick pie plate.

3 | Bake the potato crust until golden brown (around 20–25 minutes). Remove from the oven.

4 | For the filling, sauté leeks and garlic in vegetable broth over medium-high heat, until leeks are tender. Add wine and cook for about 5 minutes. Remove from heat and set aside.

5 | In a large mixing bowl, combine tofu, lemon juice, salt, bread crumbs, tarragon, thyme, mushrooms, sun-dried tomatoes, soy milk, and olives, if using. Gently fold in the leeks.

6 | Spoon filling into crust and bake for 30–35 minutes.

TIP
Wash leeks thoroughly, as they tend to be sandy inside.

COLORFUL ANTIOXIDANTS

The vibrant reds, yellow, greens, purples, and oranges of fruits and vegetables are no doubt pleasing to the eyes, but did you know that there is actually a scientific reason why food that is rich in color is also rich in nutrients? The secret is in chemicals called antioxidants, which form a protective shield around the plants' covers that protects them from potentially dangerous reactions like errant electrons and free radicals that can harm the plant. As detailed in *The China Study*, these antioxidants are usually colored and vary from the "yellow color of beta-carotene (squash), to the red color of lycopene (tomatoes), to the orange color of the odd-sounding crytoxanthins (oranges)."*

The China Study, pg. 93

MACARONI SQUASH

PREPARATION TIME: 20 minutes | **COOKING TIME:** 20 minutes
MAKES 4 SERVINGS 🍎 🌾 🐚

1 16-oz box cooked whole wheat macaroni
1 medium onion, diced
1 clove garlic, minced
2 tablespoons vegetable broth
2 cups cooked butternut squash, mashed
½ cup raw cashews
½ cup soy milk
½ cup water
2 tablespoons nutritional yeast
2 tablespoons white miso
Sea salt to taste

1 | Preheat oven to 350°F.

2 | Place cooked macaroni in a large baking dish and set aside.

3 | Sauté onion and garlic with 2 tablespoons vegetable broth in a large skillet over medium-high heat. Add squash and cook until just heated through. Add to macaroni and mix well.

4 | Process cashews, milk, water, nutritional yeast, and miso in a food processor until smooth.

5 | Pour over macaroni mixture and mix well. Season with salt. Then cover with foil, and bake for 15 minutes.

TIP

Butternut squash can be purchased both in the frozen food section and in the produce section.

MAMA'S KITCHEN PASTA WITH MARINARA SAUCE

PREPARATION TIME: 15 minutes | **COOKING TIME:** 35 minutes
MAKES 4 SERVINGS

4 tablespoons vegetable broth
2 stalks celery, chopped
1 large carrot, peeled and diced
1 medium onion, diced
4 cloves garlic, minced
1 tablespoon tomato paste
¼ cup sweet red wine
28 ounces diced tomatoes

8 ounces tomato sauce
1 tablespoon basil
½ tablespoon oregano
1 tablespoon nutritional yeast
½ teaspoon thyme
1½ cups soy crumbles (optional)
Salt and pepper to taste
16 ounces pasta, cooked

1 | Place 4 tablespoons vegetable broth in a large skillet. Add garlic, onion, celery, and carrot. Sauté on high heat until onion is translucent.

2 | Add remaining ingredients. Bring to a boil.

3 | Lower heat, cover, and simmer for 30 minutes. Season with salt and pepper.

4 | Serve over your favorite cooked pasta.

MASALA'S CHICKPEAS

PREPARATION TIME: 15–20 minutes | COOKING TIME: 20 minutes

MAKES 6–8 SERVINGS

2 tablespoons vegetable broth
1½ cups chopped onion
2 tablespoons minced garlic
2 tablespoons minced fresh ginger
1 teaspoon turmeric
1 teaspoon coriander
1 teaspoon ground cumin
½ teaspoon garam masala
2 cups diced tomatoes

2 tablespoons tomato paste
Sea salt to taste
½ teaspoon cayenne pepper (or less)
2 15-ounce cans chickpeas, drained
and rinsed
¾ cup almond milk
½ teaspoon lemon juice
4 cups cooked brown rice,
for serving

1 | In a large skillet, sauté onion over medium heat with 2 tablespoons vegetable broth, stirring frequently, until onion becomes translucent. Stir in garlic, ginger, turmeric, coriander, cumin, and garam masala. Cook for 2 minutes.

2 | Stir in diced tomatoes, tomato paste, salt, and cayenne pepper, and cook for 3–4 minutes. Stir in chickpeas, almond milk, and lemon juice. Cover and cook 8–10 minutes on low heat.

3 | Serve on top of rice.

TIPS

Coconut milk, in place of almond milk, adds a nice flavor to this dish.

The final consistency of this recipe should be thicker than a soup, more like a stew, and works well served with warmed pita bread.

MOM'S POLENTA WITH RICE AND BEANS

PREPARATION TIME: 15–20 minutes | **COOKING TIME:** 55 minutes

BAKING TIME: 30 minutes | **MAKES 6 SERVINGS**

2 cups water

¾ cup polenta

¼ teaspoon sea salt

1 small onion, diced

3 cloves garlic, minced or pressed

1 14.5-ounce can diced tomatoes

2 cups vegetable broth (I like Pacific brand—low sodium and no fat)

1 tablespoon chili powder

1 cup short-grain brown rice (sticks together better)

1 15.5-ounce can black beans, drained and rinsed

1 cup salsa

2 avocados

½ teaspoon lemon juice

¼ teaspoon garlic powder

Sea salt to taste

1 | Place 2 cups water, polenta, and salt in a medium saucepan. Bring to a boil and cook for 10–12 minutes, until polenta pulls away from the sides of the pan. Transfer to large pie dish and spread over bottom and sides of dish. Set aside.

2 | Place onion, garlic, tomatoes, broth, chili powder, and rice in rice cooker or pan. Cook rice until all liquid is gone and rice is tender (about 45 minutes).

3 | Stir black beans into the rice. Spread rice-bean mixture on top of polenta.

4 | Spread salsa on top of rice mixture.

5 | Bake at 350°F for 30 minutes.

6 | Remove from oven and set aside for 5–10 minutes.

7 | Mash avocado and toss with lemon juice and garlic powder. Season with sea salt.

8 | Arrange mashed, seasoned avocado on top of dish.

NUTTY NOODLES WITH VEGETABLES

PREPARATION TIME: 25 minutes | **COOKING TIME:** 15 minutes

MAKES 4 SERVINGS

1 pound whole wheat spaghetti or
  other pasta, cooked
¼ cup vegetable broth
1 onion, sliced
½ red bell pepper, seeded and diced
½ green bell pepper, seeded and diced
2 jalapeño peppers, seeded and diced
2 cups chopped broccoli
1 large carrot, cut in thin strips
¼ cup chopped fresh basil
2 tablespoons sesame seeds

¼ cup natural peanut butter
¼ cup light tamari or soy sauce
2 tablespoons rice vinegar,
  unseasoned
1 tablespoon minced fresh ginger
2 cloves garlic, minced
2 tablespoons agave
3 green onions, sliced
¼ cup crushed peanuts
Sea salt to taste

1 | Cook 1 pound pasta and set aside.

2 | In a large skillet, add ¼ cup vegetable broth, onions, peppers, broccoli, and carrot.
Cook for 5 minutes until vegetables are slightly cooked.

3 | Stir in pasta, basil, and sesame seeds. Set aside.

4 | In separate saucepan, add peanut butter, tamari or soy sauce, rice vinegar, ginger,
garlic, and agave. Cook over medium heat, stirring constantly, until mixture is smooth.
Pour over noodles.

5 | Garnish with green onions and peanuts. Season with salt.

TIPS

Snow peas and cauliflower are both great substitutes for broccoli.

To make beautiful and easy julienne strips of carrot, use a vegetable
peeler or julienne peeler.

PUMPKIN GNOCCHI WITH ITALIAN VEGETABLE SAUCE

PREPARATION TIME: 25 minutes | **COOKING TIME:** 25–30 minutes

MAKES 6 SERVINGS

This is a delicious and satisfying recipe that is surprisingly easy to make. The orange color of the gnocchi in contrast with the red and green of the vegetables is very appealing to the eye.

---

1 15-oz can pumpkin puree
2¾ cups whole wheat pastry flour
8–10 cups water
1 teaspoon sea salt
2 tablespoons vegetable broth
1 medium onion, sliced in long strips

1 teaspoon basil
1 tablespoon oregano
1 28-ounce can diced tomatoes
  with jalapeños
2 large zucchinis, sliced
Salt and pepper to taste

1 | Mix pumpkin and flour to make a soft dough. If necessary, add more flour so dough holds together and is not sticky. (Be careful not to overwork the dough.)

2 | Divide dough into 4–5 sections and place on a floured surface. Roll each piece into a rope about 1 inch in diameter. Cut the rope into 1-inch pieces.

3 | In a large pot, add water and salt. Bring to a boil. Add gnocchi to the boiling water and cook until the gnocchi rises to the surface and floats, about 5 minutes. Depending on the size of your pot, you may need to cook them in batches. Remove from the water and set aside.

4 | In a large saucepan over medium heat, sauté onion, 2 tablespoons vegetable broth, basil, and oregano until onion is soft, about 4–5 minutes. Add tomatoes and zucchini. Cover and cook for 5–7 minutes more, until zucchini is softened.

5 | Place vegetables on top of gnocchi and serve immediately. Season with salt and pepper.

SCRUMPTIOUS BAKED VEGETABLES WITH FRESH SPINACH

PREPARATION TIME: 25 minutes | BAKING TIME: 20 minutes

MAKES 6–8 SERVINGS 🍎 🌿 🥕 🌻 🍄

FOR THE BAKED VEGETABLES
1 medium onion, sliced
1 green bell pepper, seeded and julienned
1 sweet potato, cut into bite-sized pieces
1 head broccoli, cut into bite-sized pieces
½ pound mushrooms
1 pint cherry tomatoes, halved
1 medium zucchini, sliced
Garlic powder
Onion powder
Sea salt and black pepper
8 cups fresh spinach
2 cups cooked brown rice

FOR THE SAUCE
¼ cup balsamic vinegar
¼ cup maple syrup
¼ cup almond slivers
1 tablespoon freshly squeezed
   orange juice
1 teaspoon thyme, dried
1 teaspoon basil, dried
1 teaspoon rosemary, dried
1 clove garlic, minced

1 | Preheat oven to 425°. Prepare all vegetables except the spinach and place in a large baking pan lined with parchment paper. Sprinkle with garlic powder, onion powder, salt and black pepper. Bake vegetables for 20 minutes.

2 | While vegetables are cooking, whisk together all sauce ingredients in a medium-sized bowl.

3 | Place spinach in a large serving bowl. Combine cooked vegetables and sauce. Serve warm over spinach and brown rice.

TIP

The vegetables can also be grilled; if grilling, grill for 15 minutes instead of cooking for 25. You can prepare them up to a day in advance for quick assembly later.

MOROCCAN EGGPLANT

PREPARATION TIME: 20 minutes | **COOKING TIME:** 30 minutes

MAKES 6 SERVINGS 🍎 🥕

2 tablespoons vegetable broth
1 medium onion, chopped
4 cloves garlic, pressed
1 teaspoon ground cumin
1 teaspoon turmeric
½ teaspoon curry powder
½ teaspoon garam masala
Pinch of cayenne pepper
2 tablespoons white wine
2 tablespoons tomato paste
1 eggplant, diced (about 4 cups)

½ large green bell pepper, seeded
  and diced
½ large red bell pepper, seeded and diced
½ yellow bell pepper, seeded and diced
1 large carrot, grated
½ cup diced tomato
1½–2 cups vegetable broth, divided
¾ cup raisins
⅓ cup diced cilantro
Sea salt to taste
3 cups brown rice, cooked

1 | In a large saucepan, sauté onion, garlic, cumin, turmeric, curry powder, garam masala, and cayenne pepper in 2 tablespoons vegetable broth over medium-high heat until onion is translucent, stirring frequently. Add tomato paste and wine. Stir until browned.

2 | Add eggplant, peppers, and carrot. Stir to mix for 1 minute, then add tomatoes and vegetable broth. Cover and cook over medium heat for 20 minutes, stirring occasionally, until peppers and eggplant are soft. Remove from heat.

3 | Add raisins and cilantro. Season with salt.

4 | Serve over brown rice.

TIP

This dish is delicious served over couscous or rice.

SOUTHWESTERN CALZONES

PREPARATION TIME: 30 minutes | RISING TIME: 45–60 minutes
BAKING TIME: 20–30 minutes | MAKES 8–10 CALZONES

FOR DOUGH
4 cups whole wheat pastry flour
1 tablespoon agave
½ teaspoon sea salt
3 teaspoons instant (or bread machine) yeast
1½ cups warm water

FOR FILLING
2 cups of your favorite salsa
2 cups corn
1 can black beans
¼ cup green onions
¾ cup chopped black olives

1 | For the calzone dough, mix all the dough ingredients in a bowl. Knead with your hands for 8–10 minutes until smooth and elastic.

2 | Cut the dough into eight equal pieces. Roll dough pieces into smooth balls and place them on a nonstick baking pan about 2 inches apart. Cover with plastic wrap and set in a warm, draft-free area to rise for 45–60 minutes.

3 | Add all filling ingredients to a bowl and set aside.

4 | Preheat oven to 425°F.

5 | On a lightly floured surface, roll each dough ball out into a circle about 6–8 inches in diameter. Place 2–3 heaping tablespoons of filling in the center of the circle, wet the edges of the dough with a little water, and fold the sides together. Pinch the edges shut with your fingers or a fork.

6 | Place calzones on a nonstick baking sheet. Bake for 20–30 minutes, until tops are lightly browned.

7 | Serve hot.

TIP

These calzones can be served with Marinara Sauce (p. 191) or your favorite salsa.

SAVORY SPAGHETTI SQUASH

PREPARATION TIME: 25 minutes | BAKING TIME: 45 minutes

MAKES: 4 servings 🍎 🥕

Spaghetti squash is a dieter's dream! It has a high amount of fiber and very few calories.

---

1 spaghetti squash
¼ cup vegetable broth, divided
1 onion, diced
3 cloves garlic, pressed
4 cups diced fresh tomatoes
1 green pepper, diced
1 teaspoon rosemary

1 teaspoon oregano
1 teaspoon basil
½ teaspoon red pepper flakes
½ teaspoon thyme
½ teaspoon marjoram
1 tablespoon lemon juice
Sea salt and black pepper to taste

1 | Preheat oven to 350°F.

2 | Cut squash lengthwise and clean out seeds. Place squash cut sides down on a nonstick baking sheet. Bake for 45 minutes or until the squash is easily pierced with a sharp knife. Remove squash from oven and set aside to cool enough to be easily handled.

3 | While squash is baking, sauté onion and garlic with 2 tablespoons vegetable broth in a medium-sized skillet over medium heat until onion is soft. Add remaining vegetable broth, tomatoes, pepper, spices, and lemon juice. Cook for 5–8 minutes. Season with salt and pepper. Set aside.

4 | Using a fork, gently pull the strands of squash away from the peel. Place the strands into a large serving bowl.

5 | Add tomato mixture to squash and mix gently. Serve warm.

TIP

Spaghetti squash should be an even light yellow with no bruises. It can be stored at room temperature for up to 3 weeks and is available year-round, although its peak season is in the fall.

TOMATILLO TORTILLA BAKE

PREPARATION TIME: 15 minutes | **BAKING TIME:** 30 minutes
MAKES 8 SERVINGS 🍎 🌿 🌶

This is an easy and simple dish, great for children to prepare.

2 bags baked tortilla chips, crumbled
1 26-ounce jar of salsa
1 16-ounce bag frozen corn
1 15-ounce can pinto beans, drained
8 tomatillos, husks removed, chopped
¼ cup water

1 jalapeño pepper
½ cup cilantro
2 cloves garlic, minced
Sea salt to taste
2 avocados, chopped (optional)

1 | Preheat oven to 350°F.

2 | Place crumbled, baked tortilla chips in a mixing bowl. Add salsa, corn, and beans. Mix well. Spread in the bottom of a 9 × 12 nonstick baking dish. Cover and bake for 30 minutes.

3 | While baking, prepare tomatillo mixture. In small saucepan, add tomatillos, water, and jalapeño pepper. Cook until vegetables are soft, about 10 minutes. Pour into food processor and puree, adding cilantro, garlic, and salt to taste. Add more water if a thinner sauce is desired. Season with salt and set aside.

4 | Remove tortilla bake from oven and let cool for 15 minutes. Drizzle with tomatillo sauce and top with avocado pieces.

VEGETABLE LASAGNA

PREPARATION TIME: 20 minutes | **BAKING TIME:** 1 hour

MAKES 8 SERVINGS 🍎 🍞 🌿 🌶

1 14-ounce package extra-firm tofu
5 cups fresh spinach
4 cloves garlic
1 tablespoon dried oregano
1 tablespoon dried basil
½ teaspoon sea salt
8 cups Marinara Sauce (p. 191) (or your favorite sauce)
1 16-ounce package brown rice lasagna noodles

do ½

1 | Preheat oven to 350°F.

2 | Combine tofu, spinach, garlic, oregano, basil, and salt in food processor. Blend until smooth. Set aside.

3 | Spread ½ cup marinara sauce over bottom of a 9 × 13 baking dish. Layer with noodles, then top with half the tofu mixture and ½–1 cup marinara sauce. Top with another layer of noodles, remaining tofu mixture, and another layer of marinara sauce. Finish with a third layer of noodles and remaining sauce.

4 | Cover with foil and bake for 1 hour. Wait 10 minutes before serving.

TIP

You may add additional marinara sauce to this recipe if you like a juicier lasagna.

VEGETABLE DUMPLING STEW

PREPARATION TIME: 25 minutes | **COOKING TIME:** 35 minutes

MAKES 6 SERVINGS

FOR THE STEW
1 medium onion, chopped
2 cloves garlic, minced
4 cups vegetable broth, divided
1 tablespoon nutritional yeast
½ teaspoon oregano
½ teaspoon rosemary
½ teaspoon basil
¼ cup chopped parsley, fresh
1 cup diced potatoes

¾ cup peas
¾ cup chopped carrots
Salt and pepper to taste

FOR THE DUMPLINGS
1–1½ cups whole wheat pastry flour
½ teaspoon baking soda
Pinch sea salt
¾ cup nondairy milk
1 tablespoon agave

1 | For the stew, add onion and garlic to a large saucepan and sauté with 2 tablespoons vegetable broth over medium-high heat until translucent.

2 | Add vegetable broth, herbs, and potatoes. Bring to a boil and cook until potatoes are tender.

3 | Add peas, parsley, and carrots. Reduce heat to medium and simmer for 15 minutes, until carrots are cooked through. Season with salt and pepper.

4 | Meanwhile, for the dumplings, mix flour, baking soda, and salt in a medium-size mixing bowl. Add milk and agave, and stir until dry ingredients are moistened.

5 | Gently drop dough by rounded tablespoons into simmering stew. Cook uncovered over low heat for 10 minutes. Then cover and cook for 7–10 minutes (be sure dumplings are cooked).

6 | Serve immediately.

ZUCCHINI CRABLESS CAKES

PREPARATION TIME: 25 minutes | **BAKING TIME:** 25–30 minutes

MAKES 12 CAKES

2 tablespoons vegetable broth
½ cup chopped onion
2 medium zucchini, grated
1 cup frozen corn
¼ cup chopped parsley
1 14-ounce package firm tofu,
  drained and crumbled

¼ cup Green Garden Mayonnaise (p. 108)
2 tablespoons Old Bay seasoning
1 teaspoon sea salt
2 cups whole wheat bread crumbs
½ teaspoon paprika

1 | Preheat oven to 350°F.

2 | In large skillet over medium-high heat, add vegetable broth, onion, zucchini, corn, and parsley. Sauté until onion is translucent.

3 | In a separate bowl, combine crumbled tofu, mayonnaise, Old Bay, and sea salt. Mix well.

4 | Stir vegetables into tofu mixture. Add bread crumbs.

5 | Shape into ½-inch thick patties and place on nonstick baking sheet. Sprinkle paprika on top of patties. Bake for 25–30 minutes or until golden brown and firm when pressed in the center.

6 | Remove and let cool before serving.

TIPS

You can serve these cakes with horseradish if you like.

These cakes also make delicious sandwich patties.

SIDE DISHES

BASIL PEPPER CORN

PREPARATION TIME: 10 minutes | COOKING TIME: 10 minutes

MAKES 4 SERVINGS 🍎 🌾 🥕

---

2 tablespoons vegetable broth
1 medium onion, chopped
2 garlic cloves, minced
Cayenne pepper and sea salt to taste
4 ears raw corn, shaved (about 3–4 cups)
1 large or 2 small red bell peppers, seeded and diced
1 heaping tablespoon chopped fresh basil

1 | Over medium heat, sauté onion and garlic with vegetable broth in a large lidded skillet. When onion becomes soft, add a pinch of cayenne pepper and sea salt.

2 | Add corn, red pepper, and basil. Cover and cook 3–5 minutes.

3 | Season with more salt and cayenne pepper if needed.

TIP

The flavor of red peppers is essential for this recipe. The sweetness of these peppers works better than the flavor of green peppers.

BEETS WITH GREENS

PREPARATION TIME: 15 minutes | **COOKING TIME:** 20 minutes

MAKES 4 SERVINGS

4 medium beets
6 cups fresh greens (your choice)
1 tablespoon stone-ground or Dijon mustard
2 tablespoons lemon juice
2 teaspoons light soy sauce
1 tablespoon fresh dill (or 1 teaspoon dried dill)

1 | Wash the beets and cut off the tops.

2 | Peel the beets and slice them into ¼-inch-thick rounds. Steam over boiling water until tender, about 20 minutes.

3 | In a separate pan, sauté greens in a small amount of water.

4 | In a small bowl, mix mustard, lemon juice, soy sauce, and dill. Pour over greens and cook 2 minutes.

5 | Add the beets. Serve hot.

TIPS

Beet tops are nutritious and tasty. Young leaves make a colorful addition to salads, and more mature leaves can be steamed for a delicious vegetable side dish.

Check your local farmers' market for the wide variety of beets now being grown. Colors range from orange to red-and-white striped, and the flavors are subtly different.

CARIBBEAN MORO

PREPARATION TIME: 10 minutes | **COOKING TIME:** 40–50 minutes

MAKES 4 SERVINGS

1 medium onion, diced
3 cloves garlic, minced
½ green bell pepper, diced
½ cup cilantro, chopped
2 tablespoons Vegit seasoning (vegetable bouillon)
1 15-ounce can pigeon peas, pinto beans, or black
   beans, drained and rinsed
3 rounded tablespoons tomato paste
2½ cups water
1 cup brown rice

1 | Combine onion, garlic, green pepper, cilantro, Vegit seasoning, and ¼ cup water in a medium (3-quart) saucepan over medium-high heat. Bring to a simmer and cook until onion and pepper are soft.

2 | Add beans and tomato paste. Cook for 2 minutes. Add water and rice.

3 | Bring to a boil, then reduce heat to low and cover. Cook for 30–40 minutes, until water is absorbed and rice is tender.

CARROT BAKE

PREPARATION TIME: 15 minutes | **BAKING TIME:** 30 minutes

MAKES 4–6 SERVINGS

¼ cup vegetable broth
2 cups carrots, grated
½ cup onion, diced
½ cup celery, diced
½ teaspoon rosemary
1 teaspoon thyme
½ teaspoon salt
¼ teaspoon black pepper
2 tablespoons red cooking wine
1 cup bread crumbs
4 tablespoons Green Garden Mayonnaise (p. 108)
2 egg replacers (2 tablespoons ground flaxseed
   meal with 6 tablespoons water)

1 | Preheat oven to 350°F.

2 | In a saucepan, add vegetable broth, carrots, onions, and celery. Cook until onions are soft. Add rosemary and thyme. Remove from heat.

3 | Stir in salt, pepper, wine, bread crumbs, mayonnaise, and egg replacers.

4 | Spread mixture in a nonstick baking dish. Bake for 20 minutes, until top is slightly crisp.

CILANTRO GREEN BEANS

PREPARATION TIME: 20 minutes | **COOKING TIME:** 10 minutes

MAKES 6 SERVINGS

¼ cup water
1 large onion, diced
½ green bell pepper, diced
1 teaspoon low-sodium Vegit seasoning
   (vegetable bouillon)
2 teaspoons minced garlic
¼ cup chopped fresh cilantro
2 pounds green beans

1 | Over medium heat, sauté onion, green pepper, Vegit, garlic, and cilantro in ¼ cup water until onion is translucent.

2 | Add green beans, cover, and cook for 5–8 minutes, until beans soften. Serve hot.

TIPS

You can add other vegetables to this recipe, such as carrots and snow peas. When adding other vegetables, make sure you add more cilantro, garlic, onions, peppers, and, if desired, Vegit.

During the summer months, as I am harvesting the vegetables from my garden, I have found this recipe to work well with older, more mature green beans that for one reason or the other were not harvested when they were first ready to be picked.

CRANBERRY APPLESAUCE

COOKING TIME: 20–25 minutes

MAKES 6 SERVINGS 🍎

1 cup water
1½ cups fresh cranberries, chopped
5 cups apples, peeled, cored, and diced
8 ounces unsweetened apple juice concentrate
1 teaspoon cinnamon
Sweetener (optional)

1 | Combine all ingredients in a covered saucepan. Cook over medium heat until cranberries and apples are soft.

2 | Uncover for the last 5–10 minutes. If necessary, add more water and/or sweetener.

3 | Cool before serving.

TIPS

Use this delicious applesauce as a topping for pancakes or waffles.

This recipe can be modified by adding 3 cups of seedless red grapes in place of apples and eliminating the cinnamon.

SEE PICTURE ON PAGE 213

CREAMED CAULIFLOWER

PREPARATION TIME: 20 minutes | **COOKING TIME:** 10 minutes
MAKES 6–8 SERVINGS ✺ ◖

8 cups cauliflower florets
1 cup water
1 cup raw cashews
1 tablespoon nutritional yeast
2 tablespoons white miso
2 teaspoons Dijon mustard
1 teaspoon tahini
1 tablespoon apple cider vinegar
Freshly ground black pepper and sea salt to taste

1 | Cook cauliflower in boiling water until well done. Drain and pat dry on paper towel.

2 | Meanwhile, place water, cashews, nutritional yeast, miso, mustard, tahini, and vinegar in the bowl of a food processor. Blend until smooth.

3 | Add cauliflower to food processor and pulse 6–7 times. Do not puree. Place in a bowl and season with salt and pepper.

4 | Add salt and pepper to taste. Serve warm.

TIP

Do not place cauliflower in a Vitamix; this will over process it.

ETHIOPIAN VEGETABLES

PREPARATION TIME: 20 minutes | **COOKING TIME:** 20–25 minutes

MAKES 6 SERVINGS

2 large white potatoes, peeled and diced
2 large carrots, peeled and sliced
2 cups corn, frozen
2 tablespoons vegetable broth
1 medium onion, finely chopped
2 cloves garlic, minced
1 tablespoon ginger, minced
1 serrano pepper, seeded and minced

½ teaspoon turmeric
1 teaspoon ground cumin
1 teaspoon curry powder
1 teaspoon sea salt
1 15-ounce can diced tomatoes
1 teaspoon fresh lime juice

1 | Place potatoes in a covered medium-sized saucepan. Add enough water to cover potatoes and bring to a boil. Cook for 7 minutes.

2 | Add carrots and corn. Cover and cook for 8 more minutes.

3 | Drain the potatoes, carrots, and corn in a colander.

4 | In a large skillet with 2 tablespoons of vegetable broth, sauté onion, garlic, ginger, and serrano pepper until onions become soft. Stir in the seasonings and sauté for 1 minute more.

5 | Add vegetables, diced tomatoes, and lime juice. Cook for 7–10 minutes over medium heat, stirring frequently.

6 | Serve hot.

TIP

If possible, serve with injera, Ethiopian flatbread. However, if this is not available, use warmed tortillas or brown rice.

GARLIC GREEN BEANS AND MUSHROOMS

PREPARATION TIME: 20 minutes | **COOKING TIME:** 15–20 minutes
MAKES 4 SERVINGS

---

1 pound green beans
1 pound mushrooms
2 tablespoons vegetable broth
1 teaspoon sesame seeds

6 cloves garlic, minced
2 tablespoons tamari
Salt, to taste

1 | Rinse the beans, trim the ends, and break into 1-inch pieces. Steam over boiling water until tender, 7–10 minutes.

2 | Rinse and slice the mushrooms.

3 | Heat vegetable broth in a skillet over medium heat. Add sesame seeds and garlic, and sauté for 2 minutes.

4 | Stir in the tamari. Add the mushrooms and cooked beans. Season with salt.

5 | Cook 3–5 minutes, then transfer to a serving dish.

TIPS

The papery skins on garlic can be easily removed using a chef's knife. Lay the flat edge of the blade on top of the garlic clove and press down firmly with the palm of your hand. You should hear a slight cracking sound as the skin breaks. Then it can be easily peeled from the clove.

My mother likes green beans with tarragon. When adding tarragon to this recipe, do not add tamari or sesame seeds.

LENTILS AND GREENS

PREPARATION TIME: 10 minutes | COOKING TIME: 35 minutes

MAKES 6 SERVINGS

2 tablespoons vegetable broth
1 large onion, sliced
1 teaspoon grated fresh ginger
3 cloves garlic, crushed
1 tablespoon curry powder

2½ cups water
1 cup lentils, uncooked
2 pounds fresh greens (Swiss chard or spinach)
Sea salt and black pepper to taste
1 tablespoon lemon juice

1 | In a soup pan, sauté onion, ginger, and garlic in vegetable broth over medium-high heat until the onion is translucent. Add the curry powder and cook for 1 minute more.

2 | Add water and lentils and cook over medium-high heat until lentils are done, about 30 minutes. Once lentils are tender, add greens and lemon juice. Season with salt and pepper.

TIP

Fresh Swiss chard is usually available year-round, but you can also use kale or collard greens.

QUICK BUTTERNUT SQUASH

PREPARATION TIME: 10 minutes | **COOKING TIME:** 10 minutes
MAKES 4 SERVINGS 🍎

½ cup water
1 small butternut squash (about 4 cups diced)
2 teaspoons tamari or light soy sauce
½ teaspoon onion powder
½ teaspoon garlic powder

1 | Use a vegetable peeler to peel the squash. Then cut it in half and remove the seeds.

2 | Cut the squash into 1-inch cubes (you should have about 4 cups). Place the cubed squash into a 5-quart pot with water, tamari or soy sauce, onion powder, and garlic powder.

3 | Cover and bring to an immediate boil, then reduce heat to medium and simmer until the squash is fork-tender, about 10 minutes. You may need to add additional water. Serve warm.

TIPS

Try this recipe with other varieties of winter squash, such as delicata or kabocha. Each has its own distinctive flavor.

Winter squashes are actually grown in the summer and ripen in the fall. Because they store well, many varieties are available year-round.

SEASONED GREEN BEANS AND POTATOES

PREPARATION TIME: 8 minutes | **COOKING TIME:** 30–40 minutes

MAKES 6 SERVINGS

5 red potatoes
½ cup vegetable broth, divided
1 tablespoon Italian seasoning
1 teaspoon sea salt
2 pounds fresh green beans
1 medium onion, diced
1 teaspoon paprika
1 teaspoon black pepper

1 | Preheat oven to 400°F. Scrub potatoes and cut into ½-inch cubes or wedges. Place in bowl and coat with ¼ cup vegetable broth and seasonings. Place on parchment-covered baking sheet and roast for 30–40 minutes or until potatoes are tender.

2 | Rinse the green beans and remove the tough stems. Cut the beans into 1-inch sections.

3 | In medium skillet, add green beans, ¼ cup vegetable broth, and onion. Cook over medium-high heat, stirring occasionally, for 5–8 minutes. Add paprika and black pepper.

4 | Add cooked potatoes and turn the mixture gently as it cooks.

5 | Serve immediately.

STEWED TOMATOES

PREPARATION TIME: 15 minutes | COOKING TIME: 10 minutes

MAKES 2–3 SERVINGS 🍎 🥕

---

4 medium tomatoes, diced or blended
2 tablespoons vegetable broth
¼ cup onion, diced
¼ cup green bell pepper, diced
½ teaspoon sea salt
1 teaspoon Italian seasoning
3 tablespoons whole wheat flour
½ cup nondairy milk
Black pepper to taste

1 | Dice or blend tomatoes and set aside.

2 | Cook onion, pepper, salt, and Italian seasoning for 3 minutes in vegetable broth.

3 | Add tomatoes and continue cooking.

4 | In a separate cup, mix flour and milk until lump-free. Add to tomato mix and stir until thick.

5 | Season with black pepper.

TIP

This is good on top of your favorite toasted bread, potatoes, or biscuits.

PREVENT BREAST CANCER

In the battle against breast cancer, there are new ways to be on the offense against this ominous disease. As highlighted in *The China Study*, recent findings suggest that cutting back the amount of meat and dairy in our diets during our pre-teen and early teen years significantly reduces a woman's risk of breast cancer by reducing the hormones that can trigger it. "Several female hormones, which increase with the onset of puberty, were lowered by 20–30%…simply by having girls eight to ten years of age consume a modestly low-fat, low animal-based food diet for seven years."* Almost any type of fruits and vegetables can boost protection against cancer-related illnesses, especially cruciferous vegetables like kale.

The China Study, pg. 164

TASTY POTATOES AND KALE

PREPARATION TIME: 10 minutes | COOKING TIME: 30 minutes

MAKES 4–6 SERVINGS 🌿 🥕

4 red potatoes
½ cup vegetable broth, divided
1 bunch kale
1 onion, thinly sliced
3 cloves garlic, minced
1 tablespoon fresh dill

2 teaspoons sesame seeds
2 tablespoons lemon juice
½ teaspoon black pepper
2 tablespoons tamari
1 tablespoon ground mustard

1 | Scrub potatoes and cut into ½-inch cubes or wedges. Steam over boiling water until just tender when pierced with a fork. Rinse with cold water, drain, and set aside.

2 | Rinse the kale and remove the tough stems. Cut or tear the leaves into small pieces. Heat ¼ cup vegetable broth in large nonstick skillet and cook the kale. Set aside.

3 | Heat 2 tablespoons vegetable broth in a large nonstick skillet and add the onion, garlic, dill, and sesame seeds. Cook until onions are translucent.

4 | Add cooked potatoes and 2 tablespoons vegetable broth. Continue cooking until the potatoes begin to brown. Use a spatula to turn the mixture gently as it cooks. Add cooked kale.

5 | In a small cup, mix lemon juice, black pepper, tamari, and mustard.

6 | Add sauce to potato/kale mixture. Cover and cook, turning occasionally, for 2 minutes.

TIPS

Collard greens substitute nicely for the kale in this recipe. Both are excellent sources of calcium. However, you will need to briefly parboil the greens before adding them to this recipe.

As always, if you don't have fresh dill, this can be replaced with dill seeds.

TWICE-BAKED SOUTHWESTERN POTATOES

PREPARATION TIME: 20 minutes | **BAKING TIME:** 1 hour 20 minutes

MAKES 6 SERVINGS

FOR POTATOES

6 large russet potatoes, scrubbed and
   pricked in several spots with a fork
⅓ cup soy milk
½ teaspoon sea salt
½ teaspoon garlic powder
¼ teaspoon cayenne pepper
2 cups frozen corn
¼ cup chopped cilantro
1 15-ounce can pinto beans, drained
   and rinsed

FRESH TOMATO SALSA

6 plum tomatoes, diced
1 small onion, diced
¼ cup chopped cilantro
¼ teaspoon garlic powder
2 tablespoons vinegar
Sea salt and black pepper to taste

1 | Preheat oven to 425°F. Place the potatoes directly on the oven rack and bake for 1 hour or until soft when squeezed.

2 | Remove potatoes from the oven, cut in half lengthwise, and let stand until easily handled but still warm.

3 | Scoop out the middle of the potato into a large bowl, leaving a ¼-inch-thick shell. Place the potato shells in a nonstick 8 × 12 casserole or baking dish.

4 | With a potato masher, mash the pulp and add milk, salt, garlic powder, and cayenne. Fold in corn, cilantro, and pinto beans.

5 | Spoon mixture into potato shells. Bake for 20 minutes or until lightly browned.

6 | For the fresh tomato salsa, combine all ingredients.

7 | Serve over potatoes.

ZESTY SUCCOTASH

PREPARATION TIME: 15 minutes | COOKING TIME: 15 minutes

MAKES 4–6 SERVINGS

¼ cup water
1 small onion, finely chopped
½ large red bell pepper, seeded and diced
½ large green bell pepper, seeded and diced
1 tablespoon jalapeño pepper, seeded and minced
2 cloves garlic, minced
2 cups corn
2 cups edamame, shelled
1 15-ounce can lima beans or black eyed peas, drained
3 tablespoons red cooking wine
2 heaping tablespoons chopped fresh parsley
1 tablespoon chopped fresh basil
1 teaspoon paprika
1 teaspoon dried oregano
½ teaspoon sea salt
½ teaspoon black pepper

1 | In a large skillet, sauté onion, peppers, and garlic with ¼ cup water over medium heat.

2 | When onions become soft, add corn, lima beans (or black-eyed peas), edamame, and wine. Cook for 3–5 minutes, stirring constantly.

3 | Stir in parsley, basil, paprika, oregano, salt, and black pepper.

4 | Serve warm.

TIP

Edamame can be purchased in the frozen food section of most grocery stores, often in the health food section. This soy bean has a wonderful nutty flavor and is being substituted here for traditional lima beans.

DESSERTS

For desserts, keep in mind that a small bowl of mixed fruits is the healthiest choice of all. But, once in a while, here are some other choices to please your palate.

AMAZINGLY DELICIOUS DATE FRUIT PIE

PREPARATION TIME: 25 minutes
MAKES 8 SERVINGS 🍎 🥥

FOR CRUST
1 cup pitted dates
1½ cups walnuts (or pecans)
1 teaspoon vanilla extract
½ cup shredded coconut
½ teaspoon cinnamon

FOR TOPPING
Sliced fresh fruit (½ cup each of strawberries,
    blackberries, blueberries, mangoes, and kiwis)

1 | Blend all crust ingredients in a food processor at high speed until a paste forms.

2 | Press into a pie pan and chill until ready to add fruit.

3 | Arrange fruit on top of pie.

4 | Cool for 1 hour before serving.

APPLE GINGERBREAD UPSIDE-DOWN CAKE

PREPARATION TIME: 20 minutes | **BAKING TIME:** 35–40 minutes

MAKES 8 SERVINGS

½ cup water, divided
3 medium Macintosh (or other tart) apples, peeled, cored, and sliced
¼ cup maple syrup
1½ cups whole wheat pastry flour
½ teaspoon baking soda
¾ teaspoon baking powder
1 teaspoon ground cinnamon
½ teaspoon ground ginger

¼ teaspoon allspice
¼ teaspoon nutmeg
½ teaspoon salt
½ cup unsweetened applesauce
⅔ cup molasses
2 egg replacers (2 tablespoons ground flaxseed meal with 6 tablespoons water)
2 teaspoons vanilla extract

1 | Preheat oven to 350°F.

2 | Put apples in medium saucepan with ¼ cup water. Cover and cook 3–4 minutes over medium heat, until soft. Add maple syrup and stir to combine.

3 | In a small mixing bowl, combine flour, baking soda, baking powder, cinnamon, ginger, allspice, nutmeg, and salt. Set aside.

4 | In a separate bowl, mix applesauce, molasses, egg replacers, vanilla, and ¼ cup water. Add to dry ingredients and mix well.

5 | Spread cooked apple-maple syrup mixture evenly on the bottom of a 9 × 9 nonstick baking dish. Pour batter over apples.

6 | Bake uncovered for about 35–40 minutes, or until a toothpick inserted in the center of the gingerbread comes out clean.

7 | While cake is still warm, place a serving plate over cake pan and carefully turn the cake over so it comes out onto the plate. Serve warm.

CHEESE(LESS) CAKE WITH G-MOM'S NUTTY PIE CRUST

PREPARATION TIME: 15 minutes | **CHILLING TIME:** 2 hours

MAKES 8 SERVINGS

½ cup raw cashews
½ cup agave
1 12-ounce package extra-firm
 silken tofu
1 tablespoon xanthan gum
2 tablespoons apple cider vinegar
½ teaspoon salt

3 tablespoons tahini
2 teaspoons coconut extract
2 tablespoons vanilla extract
1 recipe G-Mom's Nutty Pie Crust (p. 258)
Fresh blueberries, sliced strawberries, and
 sliced kiwi, for topping

1 | Pour all ingredients except pie crust and fruit topping into a blender or food processor and blend until smooth.

2 | Pour the mixture into prepared pie crust and smooth the top with a rubber spatula. Refrigerate until firm and cold, about 2 hours.

3 | Spread fresh fruit evenly over the top before serving.

TIP

Other fruit toppings, such as sliced peaches, or cherry pie filling can be used on this cheesecake in place of the blueberries, strawberries, and kiwi.

CHOCOLATE BANANA PIE

PREPARATION TIME: 15 minutes | **CHILLING TIME:** 2 hours

MAKES 8 SERVINGS

¼ cup cocoa powder
½ cup Sucanat
1 cup almond milk
1 teaspoon vanilla extract
6–8 tablespoons (organic) cornstarch mixed with
    1 cup almond milk
2 medium bananas, sliced
1 recipe G-Mom's Nutty Pie Crust (p. 258)
¼ cup crushed nuts

1 | In a saucepan, add cocoa, Sucanat, and milk. Bring to a boil. Add vanilla and cornstarch mixture. Reduce heat and simmer gently for 3 minutes, stirring constantly.

2 | Layer sliced bananas on bottom of prepared pie crust. Pour mixture over bananas and smooth the top. Sprinkle with crushed nuts.

3 | Refrigerate until firm and cold, about 2 hours.

TIP

12 ounces of semisweet (dairy-free) dark chocolate chips can be used in place of cocoa, sweetener, and the sweetener-cornstarch mixture.

COCONUT MANGO PUDDING

PREPARATION TIME: 5 minutes | **COOKING TIME:** 15–20 minutes
CHILLING TIME: 2 hours | **MAKES 4 SERVINGS** 🍎

¼ cup quick cooking pearl tapioca
¼ teaspoon salt
1 15-ounce can unsweetened coconut milk
1 cup fresh or frozen mangoes, diced
½ cup Sucanat
½ cup soy milk
1 teaspoon vanilla extract
½ teaspoon cinnamon
¼ teaspoon powdered ginger
Fresh mangos and strawberries, for topping

1 | Pour tapioca, salt, coconut milk, mangos, and Sucanat into a medium-sized saucepan. Bring to a boil then immediately reduce to simmer, stirring constantly for 12–15 minutes.

2 | Add soy milk, vanilla, cinnamon, and ginger. Bring back to a boil, stirring constantly, for 3–5 minutes and then remove from heat.

3 | Pour into serving dishes and refrigerate until thickened.

4 | Garnish with mangos and strawberries.

TIP
This pudding is delicious served with your favorite vanilla wafer.

FRESH STRAWBERRY PIE

PREPARATION AND COOKING TIME: 25 minutes | **CHILLING TIME:** 2–3 hours

MAKES 8 SERVINGS 🍎 🌾

---

1 recipe G-Mom's Nutty Pie Crust (p. 258)
1½ cups sliced fresh strawberries
¾ cup water
1 cup frozen (or fresh) whole strawberries
4 tablespoons (organic) cornstarch
⅓ cup Sucanat

1 | Layer fresh, sliced strawberries on top of the graham cracker crust. Set aside.

2 | In a medium saucepan, boil 1 cup frozen or fresh strawberries in ¾ cup water until they start to dissolve. Mix cornstarch and Sucanat, and add to boiling strawberries. Boil over medium-low heat, stirring constantly, for 3–4 minutes, until mixture thickens.

3 | Once mixture is thick, pour into pie dish over sliced strawberries.

4 | Refrigerate 2–3 hours before serving.

TIP

Other fruits can be used in place of strawberries. Both blueberries and peaches work well in this recipe.

FROZEN BANANA CREAM

PREPARATION TIME: 15 minutes
MAKES 2–4 SERVINGS

FOR THE SAUCE
3 tablespoons cocoa powder
3 tablespoons Sucanat
½ cup soy milk

FOR THE BANANA CREAM
4 frozen bananas
½ cup nondairy milk
½ teaspoon vanilla extract (optional)

1 | First make the sauce by bringing cocoa, sweetener, and milk to a boil in a small saucepan. Reduce heat and cook until slightly thickened while stirring constantly. Remove from heat and set aside.

2 | In a food processor, blend bananas, milk, and vanilla until smooth.

3 | Portion banana mixture into four serving bowls. Drizzle sauce on top of banana cream and serve immediately.

TIP

Fresh fruit can be used in place of chocolate topping.

FRUIT PUDDING

PREPARATION AND BAKING TIME: 30 minutes | **CHILLING TIME:** 1 hour

MAKES 9 SERVINGS 🍎 🌾

---

4 cups mixed fruit (any combination of blackberries, raspberries,
  strawberries, pears, apples, or blueberries)
½ cup apple juice or cranberry juice concentrate
1 loaf of your favorite sweet bread (Lemon Poppy Muffins, p. 47,
  or Quick No-Fat Cranberry Bread, p. 52)
Vanilla soy ice cream, for serving (optional)

1 | Preheat oven to 350°F.

2 | Place the fruit in a large saucepan and apple juice concentrate. Simmer over low heat for 3–5 minutes. Remove from heat.

3 | Line bottom of 9 × 9 nonstick baking dish and sides of dish with slices of bread. Make sure there are no gaps between slices.

4 | Pour ½ of fruit mixture over bread. Cover top of fruit mixture with extra-thin slices of bread. Drizzle with remaining fruit mixture and press down. Cover and bake for 15 minutes.

5 | Chill in the refrigerator for 1 hour before serving. Serve with a scoop of vanilla soy ice cream.

G-MOM'S NUTTY PIE CRUST

PREPARATION TIME: 10 minutes | **BAKING TIME:** 12–15 minutes

MAKES 1 PIE CRUST

---

1 cup ground low-fat graham crackers
¼ cup ground pecans
¼ cup unsweetened, low-fat coconut
6 tablespoons applesauce

1 | Preheat oven to 350°F. Blend graham crackers and pecans in a food processor.

2 | Transfer to a bowl and add coconut and applesauce. If mixture does not form into a ball, add additional applesauce. Press into a 9-inch nonstick pie pan and bake for 12–15 minutes.

TIP

If you desire a cinnamon flavor, add 1 teaspoon of ground cinnamon.

SEE PICTURE ON PAGE 270

PINEAPPLE CHERRY CAKE

PREPARATION TIME: 10 minutes | **BAKING TIME:** 30–35 minutes

MAKES 8 SERVINGS 🍎 🌾

This is an especially quick and easy recipe.

---

1 15-ounce can crushed pineapple (not drained)
1 16-ounce can sour cherries
⅓ cup Sucanat
½ cup unsweetened coconut
1½ cups whole wheat pastry flour
½ cup agave
1 mashed banana

1 | Preheat oven to 350°F.

2 | Mix pineapple, cherries, coconut, and Sucanat. Spread in a 9 × 9 nonstick baking dish.

3 | In a separate bowl, combine flour, agave, and mashed banana. Mix until crumbly and spread evenly on top of fruit.

4 | Bake 30–35 minutes.

> **TIP**
>
> You can use fruit that is fresh, frozen, or canned. Frozen berries can be used straight from the package.

MINT CHOCOLATE PUDDING

PREPARATION TIME: 6–7 minutes | **CHILLING TIME:** 2 hours

MAKES 6 SERVINGS

1 cup cashews
1 cup water
⅓ cup maple syrup
3 tablespoons cocoa powder
2 teaspoons vanilla extract
1 tablespoon xanthan gum
½ teaspoon mint extract

1 | Add all ingredients to a food processor and blend until smooth and creamy.

2 | Cool in refrigerator for 2 hours or until thickened before serving.

TIPS

Recipes using cocoa powder tend to be much lower in fat than those using baker's chocolate.

Xanthan gum can be purchased in whole food markets and is sold by Bob's Red Mill.

MIXED FRUIT COBBLER

PREPARATION TIME: 10 minutes | **BAKING TIME:** 25 minutes
MAKES 6 SERVINGS

FOR FILLING
4 cups berries; if frozen, thaw first (use blueberries, blackberries, raspberries, or a mixture)
3 tablespoons maple syrup

FOR CRUST
1 cup whole wheat pastry flour
4 tablespoons Sucanat
1 teaspoon baking powder
½ cup almond milk

1 | For the filling, preheat oven to 400°F.

2 | In a large mixing bowl, combine berries and maple syrup. Spread in a 9 × 9 baking dish.

3 | In a separate bowl, for the crust, combine 1 cup flour, Sucanat, and baking powder. Add milk and stir to mix.

4 | Spread the mixture over the berries (don't worry if they're not completely covered) and bake until golden brown, about 25 minutes. Let cool for 10 minutes before serving.

TIP
Look for aluminum-free baking powder in your natural foods store.

PROTEIN IN PEANUTS

If you are looking to add more protein to your diet, look no further than in your kitchen pantry, where you may have a jar of peanuts stored and readily available to eat. In *The China Study*, peanuts are described as legumes that are rich in protein.*

This handy, and not to mention tasty, food choice is a convenient way to add some nutrition to your daily meals. Incorporate them in a variety of food dishes or eat them as they are, as a quick and healthy snack.

*The China Study, pg. 34

NO-BAKE PEANUT BUTTER BARS

PREPARATION TIME: 15 minutes | **CHILLING TIME:** 1 hour

MAKES 9 SERVINGS

These bars are rich, creamy, sweet, and satisfying—everything a dessert should be!

1 cup low-fat graham crackers, crushed
¼ cup crushed walnuts
½ cup reduced-fat, unsweetened coconut
⅓ cup natural peanut butter
¼ cup nondairy milk
1 cup nondairy chocolate chips
5 tablespoons rice or almond milk

1 | Crush graham crackers in food processor. In separate bowl, add walnuts, coconut, and peanut butter. Stir in crushed graham crackers.

2 | Slowly add milk and mix. If mixture does not hold together, continue adding additional milk until all ingredients stick together. However, don't make it too soft, and, if necessary, use your hands.

3 | Spread mixture evenly into a 9 × 9 nonstick baking dish.

4 | In a saucepan, melt chocolate chips together with rice or almond milk over medium heat. Stir until smooth.

5 | Spread chocolate mixture on top of peanut butter mixture. Refrigerate for 1 hour or until hardened. Cut into squares and enjoy!

TIP

These make a great holiday treat and should be used sparingly.

COCONUT OATMEAL COOKIES

PREPARATION TIME: 15 minutes | **BAKING TIME:** 15 minutes

MAKES 16 COOKIES

1 banana, mashed
1 cup nondairy milk
½ cup Sucanat
1 teaspoon vanilla
1 teaspoon white vinegar
1 cup rolled oats

1 cup whole wheat pastry flour
½ teaspoon baking soda
½ teaspoon baking powder
½ cup shredded coconut
⅓ cup chopped nuts (optional)
½–1 cup raisins or cranberries (optional)

1 | Preheat oven to 350°F.

2 | Mix banana, milk, Sucanat, vanilla, and vinegar in a small bowl.

3 | In separate bowl, mix oats, flour, baking soda, baking powder, and coconut.

4 | Add wet mixture to dry ingredients. Then mix in nuts and dried fruit.

5 | Drop tablespoon-sized amounts onto nonstick baking sheet.

6 | Bake for 15 minutes or until brown. Let cool for 30 minutes. Place cookies in a container and cover.

TIP

This recipe is also good with chocolate chips or peanut butter chips.

VEGAN CHOCOLATE CAKE

PREPARATION TIME: 10 minutes | **BAKING TIME:** 30 minutes
MAKES 9 SERVINGS

FOR CAKE
1 cup spelt flour
1 cup oat flour
½ teaspoon baking soda
1 teaspoon baking powder
¾ cup Sucanat
⅓ cup cocoa
1 ripe banana, mashed
½ cup applesauce
1 cup almond milk
1 teaspoon vanilla extract

1 tablespoon vinegar
2 egg replacers (2 tablespoons ground
   flaxseed meal with 6 tablespoons water)

FOR FROSTING
9 ounces silken tofu
½ cup chopped cashews
2 rounded tablespoons cocoa powder
¼ cup agave
1 teaspoon vanilla extract

1 | For the cake, preheat oven to 350°F.

2 | Mix flours, baking soda, baking powder, dry sweetener, and cocoa in a large mixing bowl.

3 | In a separate bowl, mix banana, applesauce, milk, vanilla, vinegar, and egg replacers. Mix thoroughly. Add to the flour mixture and mix well.

4 | Spread into a 9-inch nonstick baking pan and bake for 30 minutes, until a toothpick inserted into the center comes out clean.

5 | For frosting, while cake is cooling, combine tofu, cashews, cocoa powder, agave, and vanilla in a food processor until smooth and creamy. Spread evenly on top of cake.

SEE PICTURE ON PAGE 243

VEGAN PUMPKIN PIE

PREPARATION TIME: 10 minutes | **BAKING TIME:** 40–45 minutes
MAKES 8 SERVINGS

2 cups cooked mashed pumpkin
8 ounces silken tofu
¼ cup almond (or soy) milk
¾ cup Sucanat
1 teaspoon vanilla extract
1 teaspoon cinnamon
½ teaspoon nutmeg
½ teaspoon ginger
1 recipe G-Mom's Nutty Pie Crust (p. 258)

1 | Preheat oven to 350°F.

2 | Put the pumpkin in a food processor with tofu, milk, Sucanat, vanilla, cinnamon, nutmeg, and ginger. Process until very smooth.

3 | Pour the mixture into the crust. Bake for 40–45 minutes or until the filling is set and the crust is golden. Let pie cool to room temperature before serving.

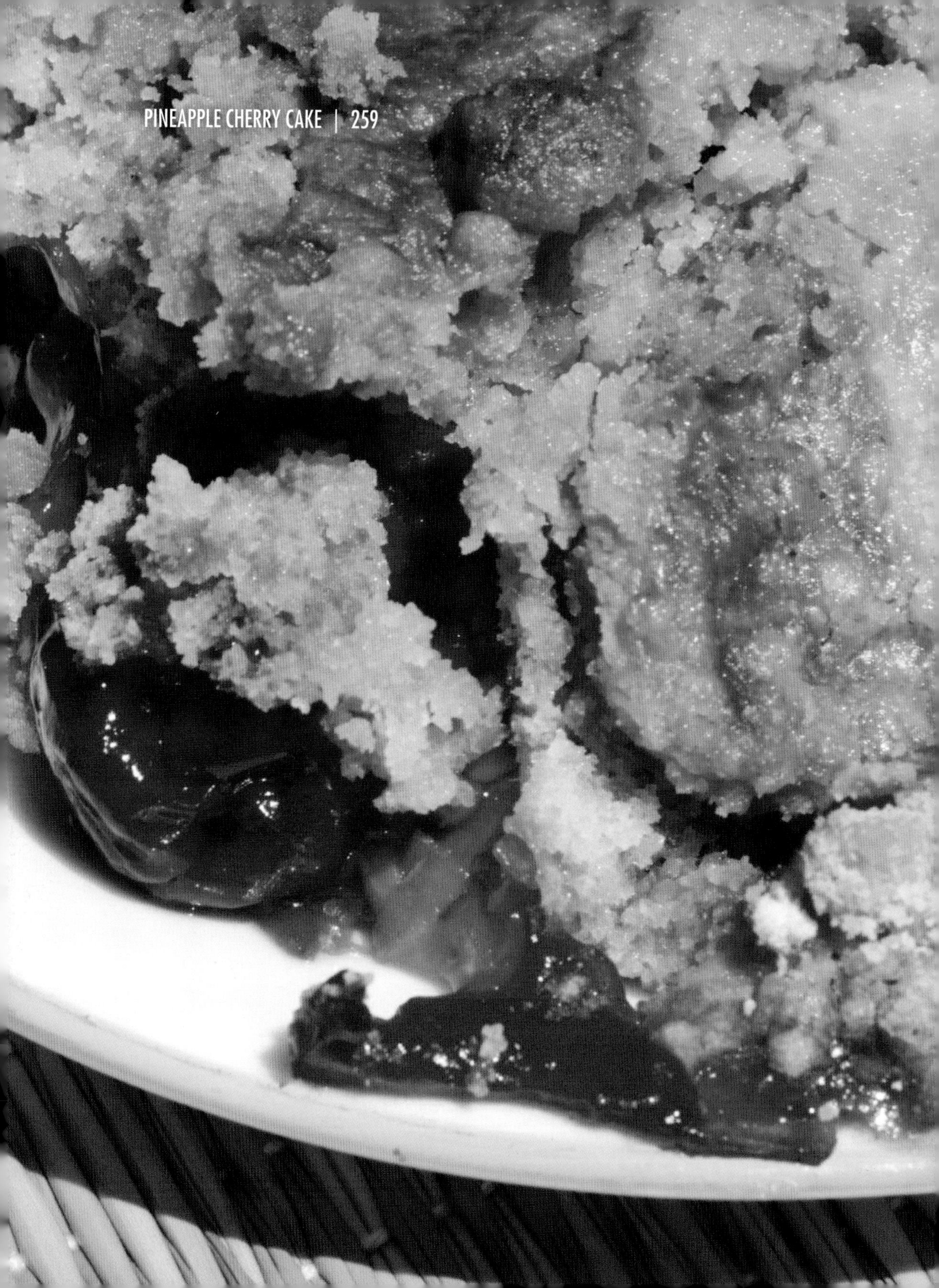

APPENDIX

METRIC CONVERSIONS

ABBREVIATION KEY

tsp = teaspoon
tbsp = tablespoon
dsp = dessert spoon

U.S. STANDARD—U.K.

¼ tsp . . . ¼ tsp (scant)
½ tsp . . . ½ tsp (scant)
¾ tsp . . . ½ tsp (rounded)
1 tsp . . . ¾ tsp (slightly rounded)
1 tbsp . . . 2½ tsp
¼ cup . . . ¼ cup minus 1 dsp
⅓ cup . . . ¼ cup plus 1 tsp
½ cup . . . ⅓ cup plus 2 dsp
⅔ cup . . . ½ cup plus 1 tbsp
¾ cup . . . ½ cup plus 2 tbsp
1 cup . . . ¾ cup and 2 dsp

DIETARY SYMBOLS

Through the use of the following symbols, each recipe in this cookbook shows which parts of the plants the dish incorporates. It's important to consume a variety of the categories each day in order to obtain all the nutrients you need.

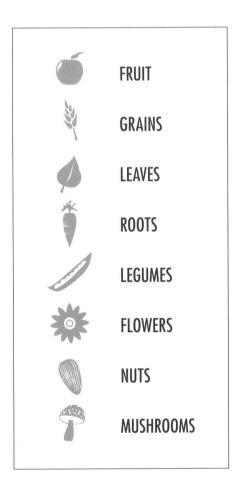

FRUIT

GRAINS

LEAVES

ROOTS

LEGUMES

FLOWERS

NUTS

MUSHROOMS

INDEX

THE CHINA STUDY COOKBOOK

ABOUT THE AUTHOR

LeAnne Campbell, PhD, lives in Durham, North Carolina. She has been preparing meals based on a whole food, plant-based diet for almost twenty years. LeAnne has raised two sons—Steven and Nelson, now nineteen and eighteen years of age—on this diet. As a working mother, LeAnne has found ways to prepare quick and easy meals without using animal products or adding oil.